Annotated Teacher's Manual

For Christian Schools

SPELLING

By Sound and Structure

2

Table of Contents

THE ROLE OF SPELLING IN A LANGUAGE

Oral communication—speaking—is the easiest and most frequently used method of communication. But oral communication has two notable limitations. Number one: It is limited by space. In the absence of electronic devices like the microphone and the telephone, a speaker's thoughts go no farther than to people within the range of his voice. Number two: Oral communication is limited by time. Without some modern invention like the tape recorder, oral communication ceases when the sound waves of a certain act of speech have ceased.

God has endowed man with a means of communication that surmounts these limitations of space and time. God gave man the ability to write. A written message can be read and understood by people miles away and by people living years after it is written.

What Characterizes a Written Language?

If writing is to communicate, the writer must follow defined patterns or acceptable practices. For example, a written language has grammar patterns; it has punctuation patterns; and it has spelling patterns. One spelling pattern or practice is this: a short *e* sound at the beginning of a word is generally written as *e,* not *ea.* One person cannot write about the *phloar* and expect another person to know that he means the same thing that that person does when he writes *floor.* If writing is to communicate, words must have standard spellings.

A written language is characterized by system, and spelling is a vital part of that system.

How Are Spelling and Reading Related?

What do spelling and reading have in common? How do they differ?

Mastering a language involves developing four related yet separate vocabularies. Even before a child can talk, he begins to understand the meaning of words that are spoken to him. These words that he understands are his *listening vocabulary.* Then as the child begins to speak and to convey his thoughts in spoken words, he develops his *speaking vocabulary.* Each month and year the number of words the child knows in each vocabulary increases. But generally throughout life the listening vocabulary remains larger than the speaking vocabulary. A person understands more words that he hears than what he himself uses to relate thoughts to others.

By the age of six or seven, most children begin to develop two more vocabularies—a *reading vocabulary* and a *writing vocabulary.* Of course, these four vocabularies overlap—for most adults the words *knock* and *syrup* and *protect* are in all four of their vocabularies. Just as the listening vocabulary is larger than the speaking vocabulary, the reading vocabulary for most people is larger than the writing vocabulary. Most people are able to comprehend more words related to a certain subject when they hear or read about that subject than what they are able to use when they speak or write about it.

Reading and spelling are language processes that use the reading and writing vocabularies. Reading is a decoding process—starting with the written word and translating it into its oral form. Spelling is an encoding process—starting with an oral word and changing it into its written form.

In order to teach spelling effectively, the teacher must understand this basic difference between reading and spelling. Reading is moving from letters to sounds. Spelling is moving from sounds to letters. The *Spelling by Sound and Structure* series is written on this premise.

How Does This Relationship Affect a Spelling Course?

A phonetic approach to reading is a superior method for teaching reading: notice the letters in the word, and sound them out in the same order they are given. But for spelling, we must reverse that process. We first hear the sounds, and then we write the letters. For example, reading phonetically says that the letters *o, o-e, oa,* and *ow* can all have the /ō/ sound. Spelling phonetically says that the /ō/ sound can be spelled with the letters *o, o-e, oa,* and *ow.* Reading phonetically says that when you see the letters *ay* at the end of a word, say /ā/. Spelling phonetically says that when you hear /ā/ at the end of a word, write *ay.**

Along with that, spelling as a decoding process affects how words are grouped for study. Reading would compare *hug* and *huge:* a final letter *g* is pronounced /g/, and the letter *g* followed by a final letter *e* is pronounced /j/. Spelling compares *hedge* and *huge:* a final /j/ sound after a short vowel sound is spelled *dge,* and a final /j/ sound after a long vowel sound is spelled *ge.*

* *A letter within slash marks indicates a phonetic sound rather than the letter name. For example, /f/ is the phonetic symbol for the first sound heard in* phrase *and* forest *and the last sound in* graph.

Can Spelling Be an Isolated Study?

Facility in a language requires skill in reading, spelling, literature, and composition, both oral and written. How much do these areas overlap—or is spelling a field all its own?

Fluency in reading contributes toward better spelling, because encountering a word often enough while reading tends to form on the mind an impression of the letters that spell the word.

Both oral reading and oral composition mean speaking—either speaking what someone else thinks or speaking what the speaker himself thinks. And speaking affects spelling. When a person says *cause* for *because* or *enner* for *enter,* correct spelling will not make much sense to him. Carefully enunciating words in the English language promotes growth in spelling ability.

In nearly every spelling class, the pupils should pronounce the spelling words aloud, distinctly. This oral practice contributes toward good spelling.

Written composition requires handwriting. Illegible handwriting and laborious handwriting hinder good spelling. Poorly formed letters could be confused with other letters: a poorly formed *d* may look like *cl,* and *n*'s without rounded humps are mistaken for *u*'s. Also, if the writer must concentrate too much on the formation of the letters, his writing slows and he loses his train of spelling thought. Handwriting skills must be taught, and then good handwriting must characterize all written work.

The lesson word lists in the grade 2 spelling books are presented in manuscript writing, since that is how the pupils likely will be writing the words. The exercises in the lessons give the pupils much practice in writing the words. Frequent writing of a word fixes its spelling in the writer's mind.

Since spelling is used in all written work, the exercises in the lessons resemble real-life writing situations whenever possible. Ultimately, spelling is useful only when applied to life's writing situations. Spelling cannot be an isolated, self-contained subject.

SPELLING AND THE ALPHABETIC PRINCIPLE

A spoken language is composed of many different sounds. Many of the sounds do not mean anything by themselves. For example, the long *i* sound by itself has a meaning, but the short *i* sound does not, and neither does the /k/ sound. Nor does just any *combination* of sounds have meaning. Slide together the three sounds /h/, /a/, and /t/, and you think of something a man wears on his head. That combination of sounds has meaning, but in reverse order the combination has no meaning: (tah). And no matter in what order you put /b/, /d/, and /g/, you cannot get a meaningful combination of sounds—you cannot get a word.

The Alphabetic Principle Defined

Consider this sentence: 2¢ + 3¢ = 5¢. That illustrates the principle of how a writing system works that uses characters to represent whole words. That sentence has eight words, hence eight characters. A writing system that uses a different character for each different word is called a *logographic* writing system (from the Greek *logos* meaning "word" and *graphein* meaning "to write").

Would not a logographic writing system be easy—write % instead of *percent,* & instead of *and,* < for *from,* and ° for *degree?* No, not easy. The English language has thousands of words; so we would need thousands of symbols, each symbol different in some way from every other symbol. It is said that the Chinese language has about 40,000 characters. Is it any wonder that the Chinese language is difficult to learn?

LC 8 6T B4 KT 8 NE. Some writing systems use a different symbol for every different syllable. This would be less cumbersome than that former system of writing symbols to stand for words (logographic writing), because usually there are fewer different syllables in a language than what there are different words. For example, the first syllable in *even* has the same sound as the last syllable in *many,* so that syllable would be written alike in both words. The first syllable in *many* sounds the same as the first syllable in *mention* and the last syllable in *amen.* That syllable would be written alike in all words in which it is heard.

The sentence at the beginning of the preceding paragraph illustrates the principle of how a *syllabic* writing system works, a writing system that uses characters to represent syllables. (American English would write that sentence like this: Elsie ate sixty before Katie ate any.)

Spoken words are made of spoken syllables. Spoken syllables are made of spoken sounds. Most writing systems in use today do not use written characters to represent entire words, nor do they use written characters to represent entire syllables. They use written characters to represent individual sounds. This principle of using characters to represent speech sounds is known as the *alphabetic principle.* Writing systems that are built on the alphabetic principle are called *alphabetic* writing systems.

A more technical term for *written character* or *written symbol* is *grapheme* (from the Greek *graphein* meaning "to write"). A more familiar term is *letter.* Letters are graphic symbols; they are written symbols; therefore, letters are graphemes.

Letters represent speech sounds. A more technical term for *speech sounds* or *spoken sounds* is *phoneme* (from the Greek *phōnein* meaning "to sound" and *phōnē* meaning "voice"). A phoneme is often called by the more general term *sound.*

The American English writing system uses letters to represent individual sounds in words. American English is built on the alphabetic principle.

The Alphabetic Principle and American English

Spelling is encoding—spelling is moving from the oral sound to the written letter. In writing systems based on the alphabetic principle, a written letter is assigned to represent a particular speech sound. In a language that has only one letter to represent each sound, the task of spelling is fairly easy. A person would first learn which letter represents each sound. Then to spell a particular word, he would simply determine the number of sounds in the word, know the order in which the sounds appear, and write their representing letters in that order. We could call that a one-to-one correspondence between sounds and letters.

In the English language there are forty or more speech sounds, depending on the system of classification used, and only twenty-six letters. So apparently some letters or combinations of letters must represent more than one sound.

Also, of the twenty-six letters in the alphabet, three letters are superfluous—they do not have any sounds of their own. The letter *c* represents either /s/, as in *cellar,* or /k/, as in *cattle.* The letter *q* represents /k/, as in *question* and *queen.* The letter *x* represents /ks/, as in *tax,* or /gz/, as in *exalt.*

It is evident that the English language does not have a one-to-one correspondence between sounds and letters. In the reading process, the letter *a* in *basket* says /a/, in *cane* says /ā/, in *hall* says /ô/, and in *above* says /ə/. In the spelling process, the /p/ sound is spelled *p* in *apron* and *pp* in *apple.* The *ough* represents four different vowel sounds in *thought, though, through,* and *bough.* In *tough* the same letters *ough* represent the vowel sound /u/ and the consonant sound /f/.

In the face of these seeming irregularities, how then can American English be called a phonetic language? How phonetic is the English language? Extensive research projects to answer this question reveal some interesting features about the language. For the majority of consonant sounds and several vowel sounds, each sound has one spelling that is used from 80 to 100 percent of the times it occurs. Examples of this are /th/, as in *thin,* spelled *th;* and /a/, as in *bag,* spelled *a.*

Many other sounds have consistent spellings in certain *positions* of the word or syllable. For example, at the end of a word, /ng/ as in *thing,* is nearly always spelled *ng.* Within a syllable, like in *think,* /ng/ is nearly always spelled *n.*

Considering phonics exclusively, about one-half of the words people ordinarily use in writing can be spelled correctly. Most of the remaining half can be spelled correctly by combining with these sound-to-letter patterns, an understanding of the word-building patterns of the language, and the word-borrowing patterns of the language. An example of a word-building pattern is that most words that end in *e* preceded by a consonant *(late, drive)* drop the *e* when adding suffixes like *-er* and *-ing,* which begin with vowels *(later, driving).*

The English language borrowed *bouquet* and *crochet* from the French language and retained the French spelling *et* for final /ā/. Numerous seemingly irregular phonetic spellings result from borrowing words without changing the spelling.

Other strange phonetic spellings are retentions of earlier spellings; over the years the pronunciation of some words gradually changed, but the spellings remained the same. The *gh* in *night* at one time was pronounced.

Actually, only about 3 percent of the words people use have such irregular spellings that they seem to follow no pattern. And in such words, often only one sound in the word has a rare spelling. In *women* only the /i/ has a rare spelling; the other four sounds are spelled with their most common letters.

The Alphabetic Principle and a Spelling Course

Since the spellings of many sounds are highly predictable, we are observing what can be called spelling patterns. When a person has observed in a number of words that a certain sound is spelled with a certain letter or letters, he begins to think in terms of that spelling pattern. He watches for that pattern in the words he is learning to spell because he knows that he can expect correspondence between particular sounds and letters.

The lessons in *Spelling by sound and Structure* cause the pupil to encounter words whose spellings follow certain patterns, and help him to apply those patterns to spell other words.

When a pupil is equipped with a workable understanding of spelling patterns, he can give his greatest attention to the maverick spellings—spellings that do not conform to any pattern he knows. When working with spelling patterns, the lessons present numerous words as examples, and then often give a word that does not follow the pattern. The spelling of that word must be memorized.

The word list for each grade determines which spelling patterns should be taught in the grade. The grade 2 lessons center on the patterns that occur most frequently in grade 2 words.

Spelling patterns are a means to an end. They should be employed when learning to spell a word only until the time that that word can be spelled without conscious thought. Just as we form letters without conscious thought of the pattern, even so with practice we spell words without conscious thought of the pattern.

The Alphabetic Principle and Enunciation

Using the alphabetic principle to spell words presupposes that writers pronounce words distinctly. Saying *travlin* for *traveling* will not help a writer to place an *e* between *v* and *l*, or a *g* at the end.

Careless pronunciation shows up in various types of spelling errors. The *traveling* example above illustrates what can happen by omitting a syllable or a sound in pronunciation. Other examples of errors caused by omitting sounds are *dentist* written as *denist* and *statute* rendered as *statue.*

Excape for *escape, subtility* for *subtilty,* and *mortal* for *moral* are examples of adding a letter or a syllable in pronunciation.

Altering the pronunciation of the vowel in the second syllables of *maintenance* and *pronunciation* accounts for the erroneous spellings *maintainence* and *pronounciation.*

Some words are spelled wrong because the writer transposes certain letters when he pronounces the words. He says and writes *pervent* instead of *prevent* and *exter* instead of *extra.*

Enunciating words distinctly will assist all writers to use the alphabetic principle to a greater advantage in spelling.

WORD LISTS FOR SPELLING

The Importance of the Word List

In his book *A Basic Life Spelling Vocabulary,* Fitzgerald asserts that the most important fundamental for the spelling curriculum is a basic word list, carefully selected and properly graded. Giving too much attention to little-used words and too little attention to frequently used words results in poor spelling ability.

Masters, in *A Study of Spelling Errors,* explains that the practical problem in teaching spelling is to aid pupils in increasing their ability to spell words which are the most likely to be used in writing in life outside the school.

The word list, then, should reflect the words the pupil writes now as well as the words he will write as an adult.

The Words for the List

The spelling word list must concentrate on the words people write.

Three categories of words should comprise the word list:

1. words written by both children and adults, like *careful* and *beautiful;*
2. words of high frequency in children's writing but of low frequency in adult writing, such as *kitten* and *arithmetic;* and
3. words of high frequency in adult writing but of low frequency in children's writing, for example, *budget* and *brethren.*

Writing vocabularies for adults include more than five thousand words. An entire spelling series can handle only two thousand to three thousand words. But which two thousand or three thousand shall it be?

Numerous research projects have been carried out in which men tabulated what words people write and how often they write the words.

To prepare our word list, we started with the most frequently used words and worked from there.

At the same time we considered the question, Is our writing as Christians not different from the writing of people in the world around us? Definitely a Christian's goals and purposes for some written work are different, but a high percentage of the words Christians use in writing are the same as those used by English-speaking people in general.

We collected word lists and scales compiled through researching child and adult writing. These lists give for each word the frequency of use and children's ability to spell it at various age levels. We collected lists of frequently misspelled words in which the difficult letters were indicated. We collected and compiled lists of religious terms relevant to the Mennonite faith.

Considering the data that the word lists and scales revealed, we were able to compile our word list for the spelling series.

Grade-placing the Words

To determine the grade level for each word, we considered the information the scales gave on the frequency of use at the different age levels. We also noted the grade levels to which other spelling series assigned the word. At each lower level, the pupil must concentrate on the words he writes at those levels. In each succeeding grade level, he learns to spell the words that he begins to use in his spontaneous writing. In addition, as the pupil advances through school, his spelling word lists should include words he will write frequently in his adult life. The overlap of child–adult writing of course is spread over all the grade levels.

The words in the grade 2 list are words that the pupil has already met. Both in reading class and in reading outside class, the pupil became well acquainted with the word—its meaning, its usage, and its pronunciation. Now in the spelling lessons, the emphasis is on his knowing how to spell it.

Grouping the Words for Practical Study

The spelling work for each grade is divided into lessons for study. Each lesson in grade 2 includes a word list of twelve words. That makes a total of 336 words in the lesson word lists.

The additional grade 2 words that could not be used in the lesson word lists are either phonetically related to words already used or words with suffixes or prefixes added to words already used. The pupils work with many of these additional words in the exercises.

What determines which words get placed in which lesson? Words could be grouped by their structure: compound words in one lesson and *-ed* past tense verbs in another lesson. Words could be grouped by their phonetic similarities: the /k/ sound in one lesson and the /j/ sound in another. Words could be grouped by common spelling difficulties: in one lesson treating words like *wrist* and *knock* that begin with what reading calls silent letters, in another lesson treating words that are often misspelled because they are mispronounced, like *memory* and *winter.* Another way to group words is by meaning relationships: number names in one lesson and carpentry terms in another. Psychologically, grouping by meanings may be a superior method; but since spelling is so highly phonetic, twelve animal names, for example, could necessitate studying ten or twelve phonetic patterns in that lesson.

Since Part B in each lesson gives practice working with a phonetic or a structure pattern, we decided that the lesson's word list should illustrate that particular pattern.

In general the words progress in difficulty from the beginning of the book to the end.

Extending the Word Lists

Not all the words a person thinks of are in the spelling word lists. But if a pupil works with the spelling patterns in the exercises and masters the words in the lists, he will be prepared to learn the spelling of any word he uses as he expands his writing vocabulary.

ORGANIZATION OF *SPELLING BY SOUND AND STRUCTURE*

Each grade's book has thirty-four lessons. Each lesson provides work for one week of school. In the book for grade 2, every lesson has two main parts, labeled PART A and PART B.

In Part A of each lesson, the pupils concentrate on the meanings of the words in the lesson word list. Since the words are already in the writing vocabularies of the average pupils in the grade, these exercises do not take the place of reading–vocabulary lessons. Part A serves to strengthen the pupil's understanding of the meanings; the pupils work with synonyms, antonyms, definitions, picture clues, context clues, and categories of words.

In Part B of some lessons, the pupils work with a phonetic pattern. In the English language there is a definite relationship between sounds (phonemes) and letters (graphemes). In the first several lessons the pupils learn to distinguish definite sounds in words. Other lessons introduce one or more speech sounds and teach the most common spellings of these sounds.

In working with sound–letter relationships, the pupils work mostly with the words in the week's word list. But they also get practice in using the spelling patterns to spell other words.

Part B of other lessons teaches how words are built—how they are structured. Next to a knowledge of phonetic patterns, an understanding of the structure of words enables spellers to spell words correctly. The word structure exercises give practice in understanding syllables and in building plurals and verb forms.

Spelling by Sound and Structure provides much review. Every sixth lesson is entirely a review lesson. And the last four lessons in each book are basically review lessons. After grade 2, each book in the series reviews from the previous book.

THE WEEKLY LESSON PLAN

	Four-day Plan		Three-day Plan
Day 1	Drill Introduce Part A Do written work A	**Day 1**	Drill Introduce Part A Do written work A
Day 2	Drill Introduce Part B Do written work B	**Day 2**	Drill Introduce Part B Do written work B Take test 1
Day 3	Drill Take test 1	**Day 3**	Drill Take test 2
Day 4	Drill Take test 2		

SPELLING DRILLS

1. Pupils print the spelling words, leaving blanks for the vowels. The pupils exchange papers and spell the words correctly, writing out entire words.
2. The teacher says words that are spelled like spelling words except for the first sound in each. The pupil says and spells the spelling word.

   For example:

   Teacher says: *brain*

   Pupil says: *grain, g-r-a-i-n*

   Teacher says: *willow*

   Pupil says: *pillow, p-i-l-l-o-w*
3. The pupils make two (or three) columns on their papers for one-syllable and two-syllable words (or for one-syllable, two-syllable, and three-syllable words). As the teacher says a word, the pupils write it in the proper column.
4. Rather than having the pupils go to the chalkboard and write isolated spelling words, dictate short sentences that include one or more spelling words.

   The boy sat on the bus.
5. The teacher says a small word. The pupil says and spells the spelling word that contains the small word.

   For example:

   Teacher says: *love*

   Pupil says: *glove, g-l-o-v-e*

   Teacher says: *ear*

   Pupil says: *fearful, f-e-a-r-f-u-l*

   Teacher says: *ask*

   Pupil says: *basket, b-a-s-k-e-t*

Caution: The teacher must avoid picking out small words in which the pronunciation changes in the big word. Seeing *eat* in *greatest, on* in *sooner,* and *cat* in *vacation* may do more harm than good in learning to spell the words.

6. Pupils write the spelling words in alphabetical order.
7. Pupils try to fit all the spelling words together crossword-puzzle style.
8. Pupils take turns saying and spelling the words in the list, one word per pupil per turn.
9. The teacher writes sentences on the chalkboard, leaving blanks for homonyms or other frequently confused words. The teacher reads each sentence aloud, including the word that belongs in the blank. The pupil spells the word.

   For example:

   Teacher writes: *We saw tiny ——— in the cupboard.*

   Teacher says: *We saw tiny ants in the cupboard.*

   Pupil says: *ants, a-n-t-s*
10. Pupils write the spelling words in syllables.
11. The pupil memorizes three or four spelling words, writes them on paper, and checks his spelling with the words in the book.
12. The teacher gives clues; the pupils select, say, and spell the words.

    For example:

    Teacher says: *It could describe a person.*

    Pupil says: *sad, s-a-d*

    Teacher says: *It tells what food can do.*

    Pupil says: *spoil, s-p-o-i-l*
13. The teacher calls out a word that rhymes with a spelling word. The pupil says and spells the spelling word.

    For example:

    Teacher says: *when*

    Pupil says: *then, t-h-e-n*
14. Instead of the pupil merely writing the word on the board, he writes a sentence about farm life, using the word.

    For example:

    The meadow fence needs to be mended in a few *places.*

    Uncle Clair threw *hay to the heifers.*

    The cornfield is beside the highway.

    OR

    Instead of the pupil merely saying and spelling the word aloud, he says the word, uses it in a sentence about farm life, and then spells it orally.

    For example:

    few *The meadow fence needs to be mended in a* few *places.* *f-e-w*

    Themes other than farm life are nighttime, school life, seeing things from a bird's viewpoint, and apples.

    For example:

    mule A mule *was tied to the apple tree. m-u-l-e*

    smooth *Feel the* smooth *skin on these apples. s-m-o-o-t-h*

    tune *Mother hummed a* tune *as she peeled apples. t-u-n-e*

WEEKLY SPELLING TESTS

After the pupil has worked with the phonetic or structure concepts in Part B, he is ready to be tested on the words in the list. The results of the test will show which words or concepts need further study.

Administering Test 1

For test 1, pronouncing the words in the same order as they are in the lesson will aid the pupils in checking their papers. Pronounce each word distinctly, use it in a short sentence, and then pronounce the word again. The pupil writes only the words.

Checking Test 1

Let each pupil open his spelling book and check his words against the words in the list. As the pupils are checking their tests, walk from pupil to pupil, checking their words. As the weeks progress, you will soon learn which pupils are more capable of checking their own papers and which pupils need your assistance.

Have the pupils write their misspelled words correctly. Assist them in further study of the words. If a mistake was caused by a failure to apply a spelling pattern, drill more on that pattern.

Record no scores from test 1; the purpose of test 1 is to give practice in spelling the words and to see where the pupils need more drill.

Administering Test 2

Even if a pupil spelled all the words correctly on test 1, he should take test 2. Words must be learned beyond the point of one successful recall.

Use the test sentences provided on pages T23–27. Pronounce the word once, say the sentence, and pronounce the word again. The pupil writes only the words.

Checking and Scoring Test 2

You will likely want to check and score test 2 yourself. Each of the twelve words is worth $8\frac{1}{3}$ percent to total 100 percent.

REVIEW TESTS

Every sixth lesson reviews the words from the preceding five lessons. To give two tests for a review lesson is unnecessary; one test is enough.

Pages T27–29 list twenty-five words each for Lessons 6, 12, 18, 24, 30, and 34. These test words were selected from the preceding lessons to illustrate the spelling patterns taught in those lessons. We selected words to cover a wide difficulty range.

Page T29 gives a suggested list of twenty-five words to use as a final test at the end of the year. These words were selected from all of the lessons in the book and cover a wide difficulty range. They also illustrate many of the spelling patterns taught in the book.

INTRODUCING THE LESSONS

These pages give suggestions for introducing the lessons to the pupils.

The additional activity suggested in many of the lessons can be assigned to the entire class at the teacher's discretion, or it can be assigned only to the more capable students. The teacher can write the directions on the chalk board or duplicate a copy for each pupil.

Lesson 1

Introducing Part A

Most pupils in grade 2 are familiar with all twelve spelling words and use them freely in their oral communication. If you realize that any word is unfamiliar to a pupil, discuss its meaning to acquaint the pupil with it.

Have the pupils look at the word list on page 4. As you say each word aloud, have them follow along and pronounce it after you.

Listen to be sure that the pupils pronounce the initial /b/ and /p/ sounds correctly. Since the lips are held in the same position to say both sounds, some children confuse the two sounds. The /b/, however, uses the voice box, but the /p/ does not.

Listen also to initial /d/ and /t/. The tongue and the upper gum ridge are used to articulate both /d/ and /t/. However, like /b/, /d/ uses the voice box. And like /p/, /t/ does not use the voice box.

For more practice in saying the spelling words, help the pupils to use each word in an oral sentence.

Assign Part A.

Introducing Part B

Direct the pupils to open their books to Lesson 1 and to look at the picture at the top of page 4. What spelling words do they think of when they see this picture? At least these three should be mentioned: *cap, rain,* and *hat.* Let pupils mention other words too if they have logical reasons to give, such as "The boy is bearing a *big* cap."

Focus attention now on one word at a time that was mentioned. Have the class say it and listen for the first sound—the beginning sound—in the word. Then think what letter spells that sound. For example, say *cap* aloud. The beginning sound is /k/. The /k/ sound is spelled with the letter *c.*

Say some other words that begin with that particular sound, and let the pupils suggest what letter spells the beginning sound in each.

cap	*rain*	*hat*
card	*row*	*hand*
came	*ran*	*hog*
cats	*red*	*hay*

Have the pupils look at the word list on page 4. Say the words with the pupils.

Assign Part B on page 5.

Additional Activity:

Write three sentences about the picture at the top of page 4.

In the first sentence, tell the names of the boys.

In the second sentence, tell what each boy is wearing on his head.

In the third sentence, tell what is falling from the sky.

Lesson 2

Introducing Part A

Most pupils in grade 2 are familiar with all twelve spelling words and use them freely in their oral communication. If you realize that any word is not familiar to a pupil, discuss its meaning to acquaint the pupil with it.

Have the pupils look at the word list on page 6. As you say each word aloud, have them follow along and pronounce it after you.

For more practice in saying the spelling words, encourage the pupils to use each word in an oral sentence.

Assign Part A.

Introducing Part B

Have the pupils open their books to Lesson 2 and look at the picture at the top of page 6. What spelling words do they think of when they see this picture? At least these three should be mentioned: *top, can,* and *nut.*

Focus attention on one word at a time that was mentioned. Have the class say it and listen for the beginning sound and then for the second sound. Think what letter spells each second sound.

Say some other words that have the same second sound, and let the pupils suggest what letter spells that sound.

top	*can*	*nut*
box	*bad*	*jump*
lots	*lap*	*runs*
job	*has*	*gum*

Have the pupils look at the word list on page 6. Say the words with the pupils.

Assign Part B on page 7.

Additional Activity:

Write three sentences about the picture at the top of page 6.

In the first sentence, tell what is on the table.

In the second sentence, tell what we can do with nuts.

In the third sentence, tell if you like to eat nuts.

Lesson 3

Introducing Part A

Most pupils in grade 2 are familiar with all twelve spelling words and use them freely in their oral communication. If you realize that any word is unfamiliar to a pupil, discuss its meaning to acquaint the pupil with it.

Have the pupils look at the word list on page 8. As you say each word aloud, have them follow along and pronounce it after you.

For more oral practice with the spelling words, let the pupils use each word in a sentence.

Assign Part A.

Introducing Part B

Tell the pupils to look at the pictures at the top of page 8. Does anyone know what the first picture is? *(horn)* Ask what noise a horn makes. Sometimes we say that a horn says *Toot, toot.* Does someone know another noise that a horn can make? *(beep)* Say *beep* several times and listen for the beginning sound.

What is the second picture? *(chick)* Ask what noise a chick makes. *(peep)* Say *peep* several times and listen for the beginning sound. Is it the same as the beginning sound in *beep?*

Which spelling word sounds like *beep* and *peep* except for the beginning sound? *(keep)*

Give practice in hearing and saying words with the beginning sound /b/ and /p/, and /d/ and /t/. Some children have difficulty distinguishing these sounds.

be	*pea*	*door*	*tore*
bar	*pan*	*draw*	*tea*
bills	*pills*	*dolls*	*told*
boats	*part*	*down*	*town*

Say aloud with the pupils the spelling words on page 8.

Assign Part B on page 9.

Lesson 4

Introducing Part A

If you think that any word in the list may be unfamiliar to a pupil, discuss its meaning to acquaint the pupil with it.

Have the pupils look at the word list on page 10. As you say each word aloud, have them follow along and pronounce it after you.

Take care to pronounce the final sound in each word. Watch, however, that you do not overarticulate to the extent that you say an /u/ sound after the consonant. Say only /d/ or /n/ or /s/, as the case may be, not /du/ or /nu/ or /su/.

For more oral practice with the spelling words, have the pupils use each word in a sentence.

Assign Part A.

Introducing Part B

Tell the pupils to look at the pictures at the top of page 10. What words do they think of that begin with the letters *h-o-o*? *(hood, hook, hoop, hoot)* Which of those words is a spelling word? *(hook)* Focus attention on the last sounds in these *h-o-o* words, and think about what letters spell those sounds.

Ask the pupils to say another word that begins with *h-o-o*. (Thinking about a horse might be a clue: *hoof.)*

Say some other words, and let the pupils suggest what letter spells the last sound in each.

than *tent* *walk* *hard* *hog*

Say aloud with the pupils the spelling words on page 10.

Assign Part B on page 11.

Lesson 5

Introducing Part A

Have the pupils look at the word list on page 12. As you say each word aloud, have them follow along and pronounce it after you.

Do your pupils frequently say "I seen" for "I saw"? Encourage the pupils to use each spelling word in an oral sentence, beginning each sentence with "I saw."

Assign Part A.

Introducing Part B

Have the pupils turn to page 12 and look at the picture at the top of the page. Does someone know what it is? *(a traffic light)* Mention that the top light is red and the middle light is yellow. Let someone tell you the color of the bottom light. *(green)*

Which of these colors—red, yellow, or green—is a spelling word? *(green)* When the traffic light shows the green light, what do we do? *(We go.)* Which spelling word tells us what we do when the red light shines? *(stop)*

Focus attention on *green* and *stop,* one word at a time. Listen for the first two sounds in each word and think about what letters spell these sounds.

Write the term *consonant blend* on the chalkboard. Help the pupils to say it several times, and state that *gr* and *st* are consonant blends. (If your pupils do not know what vowels are and what consonants are, explain that first. Most second graders do know.)

Say some other words, and let the pupils suggest what the consonant blend is in each.

store *trip* *sled* *draw* *bring*

Say aloud with the pupils the spelling words on page 12.

Assign Part B on page 13.

Additional Activity:

Write three sentences about the picture at the top of page 10.

In the first sentence, tell where traffic lights are found.

In the second sentence, tell what colors a traffic light has.

In the third sentence, tell what we do when the red light shines.

Lesson 7

Introducing Part A

Most pupils in grade 2 are familiar with all twelve spelling words and use them freely in their oral communication. If you think that any word may be unfamiliar to a pupil, discuss its meaning to acquaint the pupil with it.

Have the pupils look at the word list on page 16. As you say each word aloud, have them follow along and pronounce it after you.

For more practice in saying the spelling words, help the pupils to use each word in an oral sentence.

Assign Part A.

Introducing Part B

Turn to page 16 and discuss the illustration at the top of the page. The first picture shows one man. The second picture shows three men. What *sound* is different in the words *man* and *men?*

Help the pupils to hear this same difference in *bad* and *bed* and in *pan* and *pen.*

In the illustration at the top of the page, what *letter* is needed in the word to spell *man?* What letter is needed to spell *men?*

Write the following words on the chalkboard, drawing a blank in place of every vowel. Say one word at a time. Have the pupils repeat the word and tell what letter spells the vowel sound.

bag	*sand*	*camp*	*ask*	*end*
beg	*send*	*has*	*leg*	*sent*

Say aloud with the pupils the spelling words on page 16.

Assign Part B on page 17.

Lesson 8

Introducing Part A

Pronounce the spelling words clearly for the pupils while they look at the word list on page 18 and say each word after you.

For more practice in saying the spelling words, encourage the pupils to use each word in a sentence. You can also give practice in saying "I saw" instead of "I seen" by asking that every sentence begin with "I saw."

Assign Part A.

Introducing Part B

Discuss the illustration at the top of page 18. Help the pupils to say the words *ship* and *chip* distinctly. For pupils to spell the digraphs /sh/ and /ch/ correctly in words, they must be able to hear the difference and say the digraphs clearly.

Which of these two words—*ship* or *chip*—is a spelling word? What two letters spell the first sound in *ship?* Mention that the letters *sh* are a *digraph* when they spell the first sound you hear in *ship.*

The letters *ch* are another digraph when they spell the first sound in *chip.*

Say the following words one at a time. Have the pupils repeat the word and say the letters *ch* or *sh* to tell what letters spell the first sound.

shirt	*showing*	*chase*	*short*
cherry	*chin*	*Sharon*	*Charles*

Say aloud with the pupils the spelling words on page 18.

Assign Part B on page 19.

Lesson 9

Introducing Part A

As you pronounce the spelling words on page 20, be careful not to make the mistake of adding an /u/ sound after every consonant digraph. The pupils should look at the word list in their books and pronounce each word after you.

For more oral practice with the spelling words, let the pupils use each word in a sentence.

Assign Part A.

Introducing Part B

Do the pupils recall that in Lesson 8 they studied words that began with consonant digraphs? Let the pupils volunteer the four digraphs /ch/, /sh/, /th/, and /th/, spelled *ch, sh,* and *th.* Do the spelling words in Lesson 9 *begin* with these sounds? No, they *end* with digraphs.

Discuss the illustration at the top of page 20. What spelling word does the first picture make them think of? *(wash)* What word names the second picture? *(watch)* Be sure the pupils can hear the difference in these ending sounds.

Explain that the two letters *sh* spell the last sound in *wash* and that the three letters *tch* spell the last sound in *watch.* The pupils will notice as they study this lesson that the ending /ch/ sound is spelled *ch* in some words and *tch* in other words.

Say aloud with the pupils the spelling words on page 20.

Assign Part B on page 21.

Lesson 10

Introducing Part A

If you think that any word in the list may be unfamiliar to a pupil, discuss its meaning to acquaint the pupil with it.

Have the pupils look at the word list on page 22. As you say each word aloud, have them follow along and pronounce it after you. Be careful to say /t/, not /d/, in *little*. The words *sun* and *son* are pronounced alike.

For more oral practice with the spelling words, let the pupils say sentences that use the spelling words.

Assign Part A.

Introducing Part B

Turn to the illustration at the top of page 22. Let the pupils tell which spelling words the picture reminds them of. *(hot, sun)* The words *hot* and *sun* both have short vowel sounds in them.

The words in Lesson 7 had the short vowel sounds /a/ and /e/. Every word in Lesson 10 has either /i/, /o/, or /u/. Say each spelling word distinctly. Have the pupils repeat it clearly and tell which short vowel sound they hear. In the words *front* and *son,* do not let the vowel spellings mislead the children. The vowel sound in both these words is /u/.

Assign Part B on page 23.

Additional Activity:

Write three sentences about the picture at the top of page 22.

In the first sentence, tell what you see in the picture.

In the second sentence, tell what the sun does.

In the third sentence, tell how you feel about the sun.

Lesson 11

Introducing Part A

Pronounce the spelling words clearly for the pupils while they look at the word list on page 24 and say each word after you.

For more practice in saying the spelling words, encourage the pupils to use each word in a sentence. If your pupils frequently make a grammatical error, like saying "I seen" instead of "I saw" or "We brang" instead of "We brought," you could use this exercise to give practice in saying the correct form by using the correct form in every sentence.

Assign Part A.

Introducing Part B

Have the pupils turn to page 24 in their books. Can someone tell you what is pictured at the top of the page? *(money—three coins—a penny, a nickel, and a dime)* Which of these three coin names is a spelling word? *(dime)*

If we have money and need to buy something, we *(spend)* the money. Which spelling word tells what we do with money when we do not spend it? *(save)*

Review the short vowel sounds: /a/, /e/, /i/, /o/, /u/. Say the long vowel sounds together: /ā/, /ē/, /ī/, /ō/, /ū/.

Say the following words one at a time. Have the pupils say each word after you and tell if they hear /ā/, /ē/, /ī/, /ō/, or /ū/. As the pupils mention the vowel sounds, write the words on the chalkboard.

came	mule	five	game
hike	Eve	Jane	woke

Help the pupils to hear that in every word on the board the long vowel sound is the next-to-last sound in the word. Mention that the *e* at the end of the word helps to spell the long vowel sound.

Say aloud with the pupils the spelling words on page 24.

Assign Part B on page 25.

Additional Activity:

Write three sentences about the picture at the top of page 24.

In the first sentence, tell what you see in the picture.

In the second sentence, tell one thing we can do with it.

In the third sentence, tell something else we can do with it.

Lesson 13

Introducing Part A

Have the pupils look at the word list on page 28. As you pronounce each word aloud, have them follow along and pronounce it after you.

For more practice in saying the words, help the pupils to use each word in an oral sentence.

Assign Part A.

Introducing Part B

Have the pupils open their books to page 28 and look at the picture at the top of the page. What spelling words do they think of as they observe the picture? *(seats, arms, boys, heads)*

Tell the pupils to place their right hand over the boy who is walking. Now what do they see? *(one seat, one boy, one head, and one arm)* Say to the pupils, *"Seat, boy, head, arm.* A word that names *one* person or thing is a *singular noun.* Remove your hand from the picture. *Seats, boys, heads, arms.* A word that names *more than one* person or thing is a *plural noun."*

As you together say the spelling words on page 28, first say the singular form and then the plural form, like this: road, roads; seat, seats; train, trains; and so forth. Ask what letter at the end of every spelling word tells us that the word means more than one person, place, or thing. *(s)*

Assign Part B on page 29.

Additional Activity:

Write three sentences about the picture at the top of page 28.

In the first sentence, tell the name of the one boy and tell what he is doing.

In the second sentence, tell the name of the other boy and tell what he is doing.

In the third sentence, tell what the boys will talk about as they visit.

Lesson 14

Introducing Part A

As you say the spelling words, have the pupils look at the word list on page 30 and pronounce each word after you.

For more practice in saying the words, help the pupils to use each word in an oral sentence. Begin each sentence with "He doesn't" to give practice using "He doesn't" rather than "He don't."

Assign Part A.

Introducing Part B

Ask what a word is called that names one person or thing. *(singular noun)* Ask what a word is called that names two or more people or things. *(plural noun)*

Write *car, hill,* and *boat* in a column on the chalkboard. "These are singular nouns. First say the singular noun as I point to it. Then spell it. Next say the plural noun and spell it." Write each plural form on the chalkboard as it is given. Ask what letter shows that the word means more than one person or thing. *(s)*

Have the pupils open their books to page 30 and look at the picture at the top of the page. What spelling words does the picture make them think of? *(cows, bushes)* Write *cows* and *bushes* on the chalkboard. Help the pupils to hear and say the *-s* and *-es* endings. Tell them that when we say the syllable /ez/ to make a word plural, we must spell it with the letters *es.*

Say with the pupils the spelling words on page 30.

Assign Part B on page 31.

Additional Activity:

Write three sentences about the picture at the top of page 30.

In the first sentence, tell what you see in the picture.

In the second sentence, tell what cows like to do.

In the third sentence, tell where the cows will go at milking time.

Lesson 15

Introducing Part A

If you think that any word in the list may be unfamiliar to a pupil, discuss its meaning to acquaint him with it.

Say aloud the words in the list on page 32, with the pupils following along and pronouncing each word after you. In *hunted* and *started* be sure to pronounce the *t* at the end of both root words. You will want to be careful to pronounce the *-ed* suffix as /ed/, /d/, or /t/, as the case may be, but not to overenunciate by adding an /u/ sound at the end of the word.

For more practice in saying the words, help the pupils to use each word in an oral sentence.

Assign Part A.

Introducing Part B

Let the pupils study the picture at the top of page 32. Tell them to make up a sentence using a spelling word and telling about the picture. Help the pupils, if necessary, to give sentences like these:

The girl washed *the dishes.*
The girl worked *in the kitchen.*
The girl helped *her mother.*
The girl turned *away from the sink.*

What two letters at the end of every spelling word tell us that something did happen? *(ed)*

As you together say the spelling words, first say each word without *-ed* and then say it with *-ed,* like this: *hunt, hunted; start, started;* and so forth.

Assign Part B on page 33.

Additional Activity:

Write three sentences about the picture at the top of page 32.

In the first sentence, name the girl and tell what she did.

In the second sentence, tell why the girl is happy.

In the third sentence, tell what you think the girl will do next.

Lesson 16

Introducing Part A

Pronounce each spelling word on page 34 for the pupils while they follow along and say each word after you. It is easier to include the ending /g/ sound when you say words in a list like this than when you say the same words in sentence context. As you help the pupils to use each spelling word in an oral sentence, give attention to the ending /g/ sound.

Assign Part A.

Introducing Part B

Have the pupils turn to page 34 and look at the picture. Say, "Pretend you are looking out the window and this is what you see. You might say, 'Look, it is . . .' What spelling word might you say?" *(snowing)* "Or, you might say, 'Look, snowflakes are . . .' " *(falling)*

What three letters at the end of every spelling word tell us that something is happening right now? *(ing)*

As you together say the spelling words, first say each word without *-ing* and then say it with *-ing,* like this: *read, reading; sing, singing;* and so forth.

Assign Part B on page 35.

Additional Activity:

Write three sentences about the picture at the top of page 34.

In the first sentence, tell what is in the picture.

In the second sentence, tell what season of the year it is.

In the third sentence, tell something about snow.

Lesson 17

Introducing Part A

Discuss the meaning of any word that may be unfamiliar to your pupils.

Have the children follow along in the word list on page 36 as you pronounce each word for them and they say it after you.

For more practice in saying the words, help the pupils to use each word in an oral sentence.

Assign Part A.

Introducing Part B

Saying and spelling words by syllables is a help in spelling words correctly.

Write the following words on the chalkboard. Pronounce each one for the pupils. As you say each word, let your finger tap your desk or the chalkboard once at the exact time that you say the word: *hats, gas, card, ways, than, the.*

Next repeat the exercise, having the pupils say the words with you and tap their desks at the same time that you tap.

Then write this next set of words on the board. As you say each word for the pupils, let your finger tap your desk twice—once with each syllable: *apple, finding, rivers, sister, wishes.* Remember to accent the accented syllable just as you would in normal speaking.

Then repeat the exercise, having the pupils say the words with you and tap their desks at the same time you tap. This helps the pupils to hear and feel the syllables.

Have the pupils turn to page 36 and observe the picture. What spelling words does the picture make them think of? *(wagon, wood)*

This time when you say the spelling words aloud with the pupils, both you and they should tap once with each syllable.

Assign Part B on page 37.

Additional Activity:

Write three sentences about the picture at the top of page 36.

In the first sentence, tell who loaded the wagon and what he put on the wagon.

In the second sentence, tell what the person will do with what is on the wagon.

In the third sentence, tell how the person feels about what he is doing.

Lesson 19

Introducing Part A

If you think that any words might be unfamiliar to your pupils, discuss their meanings with the class.

The pupils should follow along in the word list on page 40 and say each word aloud after you. Try to accent *asleep* and *afraid* on the second syllable, as we do in normal sentence speaking.

To give the pupils more practice in saying the words, help them to use each word in an oral sentence.

Assign Part A.

Introducing Part B

As the class turns to page 40 in their books, have them recite together the long vowel sounds: /ā/, /ē/, /ī/, /ō/, /ū/. Mention that in this lesson we will study the /ā/ and /ē/ sounds.

What spelling words does the picture at the top of the page make them think of? The pupils should mention at least these four: *gate, leaf, asleep, mail.*

Some words sound alike except for the /ā/ and /ē/ sounds. Have everyone say *hay* and *he* with you. Write the two words on the board. Underline the *h* in both words. Circle *ay* and *e,* the letters that spell the /ā/ and /ē/ sounds. Do the same with *laid* and *lead,* underlining the *l* and *d* in both words and circling *ai* and *ea.*

Write *me* on the board. Ask which spelling word sounds like *me* except that it has the /ā/ sound instead of the /ē/ sound. *(may)* Ask which two spelling words are alike except for the vowel sounds. *(meal, mail)*

Say with the pupils the spelling words on page 40.

Assign Part B on page 41.

Additional Activity:

Write three sentences about the picture at the top of page 40.

In the first sentence, tell something about the dog.

In the second sentence, tell something about the gate.

In the third sentence, tell something about the mailbox.

Lesson 20

Introducing Part A

Have the pupils turn to page 42 and follow along as you say the words in the list and they pronounce each word after you.

To give the pupils more practice in saying the words, help them to use each word in an oral sentence.

Assign Part A.

Introducing Part B

As the pupils turn to page 42 in their books, recite with them the long vowel sounds: /ā/, /ē/, /ī/, /ō/, /ū/. Mention that in this lesson we will study the /ī/ and /ō/ sounds.

Do any of the pupils, or people the pupils know, have names containing /ī/ or /ō/? Write a few names on the board and underscore the spellings of the /ī/ and /ō/ long vowel sounds. For example, Rhoda, Rose, Joseph, Joel, Michael, Titus, Dwight.

What spelling words does the picture at the top of the page make them think of? Pupils should mention at least *blow* and *light*.

Say with the pupils the spelling words on page 42.

Assign Part B on page 43.

Additional Activity:

Write three sentences about the picture at the top of page 42.

In the first sentence, tell something about the girl.

In the second sentence, tell something else about the girl.

In the third sentence, tell something about the candle.

Lesson 21

Introducing Part A

Pronounce the spelling words on page 44 while the pupils follow along in their books and say each word after you.

To give the pupils more practice in saying the words, help them to use each word in an oral sentence. For a special challenge, see if they can use the first two words in the same sentence, the next two in another sentence, and so on.

Assign Part A.

Introducing Part B

Tell the pupils to turn to page 44. Say the spelling words aloud with them.

Now tell them to think about the spelling words as they study the picture at the top of the page. We could call the woman a ———. *(cook)* The cook is stirring ——— in the kettle. *(food)* The kettle is not empty; it is nearly ———. *(full)*

Can the students make up more sentences about the picture, using spelling words? For example: The cook *looked* into the kettle. The cook *took* a spoon to stir the food.

Mention that in this lesson we are learning to spell the vowel sounds /oo/ and /o͞o/. Have the pupils say all the spelling words again and after each one tell if it contains /oo/ or /o͞o/.

Assign Part B on page 45.

Additional Activity:

Write three sentences about the picture at the top of page 44.

In the first sentence, tell who the person is and where she is.

In the second sentence, tell what she is doing.

In the third sentence, tell why she is doing what she is.

Lesson 22

Introducing Part A

Say aloud the words in the list on page 46. Have the pupils pronounce each word after you.

To give the pupils more practice in saying the words, help them to use each word in an oral sentence. You could begin each sentence with a pupil's name.

Assign Part A.

Introducing Part B

Have the pupils turn to page 46 and look at the picture at the top of the page. Say, "Let's call this girl Sandra." Write on the board, "Sandra ____ glasses." Ask what spelling word belongs in the blank. *(needs)* Then say or write this sentence and ask what spelling word fits in the blank: "Sandra ____ better with glasses than without them." *(sees)*

What letter at the end of every spelling word tells us that something is happening now *(s)*

As you together say the spelling words, first say each word without the *-s* suffix and then say it with *-s,* like this: *like, likes; take, takes;* and so forth.

Assign Part B on page 47.

Additional Activity:

Write three sentences about the picture at the top of page 46.

In the first sentence name, the person and tell how old she is.

In the second sentence, tell what new thing she has on her face.

In the third sentence, tell why she is smiling.

Lesson 23

Introducing Part A

If you think that any word may be unfamiliar to your pupils, discuss its meaning to acquaint them with it.

Say aloud the words in the list on page 48. Have the pupils pronounce each word after you.

To give the pupils more practice in saying the words, help them to use each word in an oral sentence.

Assign Part A.

Introducing Part B

Tell the pupils to look at the picture at the top of page 48. What spelling words does the picture make them think of? They should mention at least these: *words, learn, working, paper.*

Mention that in this lesson we are studying the /ėr/ sound and that /ėr/ is spelled with one or two vowels plus *r.* Say aloud with the pupils one spelling word at a time. After each, tell the pupils that letters spell the /ėr/ sound in that word.

Assign Part B on page 49.

Additional Activity:

Write three sentences about the picture on page 48.

In the first sentence, name the person and tell where he is.

In the second sentence, tell what he is doing.

In the third sentence, tell how he is doing his work.

Lesson 25

Introducing Part A

As you say each word in the list aloud, have the pupils follow along on page 52 and pronounce each word after you. For more practice in saying the words, help the pupils to use each word in an oral sentence.

Assign Part A.

Introducing Part B

Have the pupils look at the picture at the top of page 52. Say, "This is the wall of a house. This wall is made of two kinds of building material. Both kinds are spelling words in this lesson. Do you know what they are?" *(block, brick)*

Ask what sound ends both *block* and *brick.* (/k/) In both these words /k/ is spelled with the letters *ck.*

The /k/ sound is not always spelled *ck.* Say aloud with the pupils the spelling words, one at a time. Listen for the /k/ sound in each word. Decide whether the /k/ sound is the first sound, is the last sound, or comes within the word. And notice what letter or letters spell /k/ in every word. (Observe that *kick* has two /k/ sounds.)

Assign Part B on page 53.

Additional Activity:

Write three sentences about the picture at the top of page 52.

In the first sentence, tell what building we are looking at.

In the second sentence, tell why the windows are sparkling clean.

In the third sentence, tell what is growing beside the building.

Lesson 26

Introducing Part A

Pronounce the spelling words clearly for the pupils while they look at the word list on page 54 and say each word after you. Watch that the last word, *once,* is not ended with a /t/ sound.

For more practice in saying the spelling words, encourage the pupils to use each word in a sentence.

Assign Part A.

Introducing Part B

Direct the pupils to the picture at the top of page 54. Ask, "Who can tell us what is slithering through the grass?" *(a snake)* "Everyone say *snake.* What is the first sound in *snake?*" (/s/)

"Do you know how to spell *snake?* What letter spells the first sound?" *(the letter* s) "The snake in the picture even looks like the letter *s,* doesn't it?"

Write the following words on the chalkboard. Let the class tell you what letter or letters spell the /s/ sound in every word, and underscore those letters.

see *face* *glass* *cent*
fast *rice* *guess* *circle*
wants

Say aloud with the pupils the spelling words on page 54.

Assign Part B on page 55.

Additional Activity:

Write three sentences about the picture at the top of page 54.

In the first sentence, tell where you were walking.

In the second sentence, tell what you saw in the grass.

In the third sentence, tell what the snake did.

Lesson 27

Introducing Part A

Pronounce the spelling words clearly for the pupils while they look at the word list on page 56 and say each word after you. Give attention to the beginning /hw/ and /w/ sounds.

For more practice in saying the spelling words, encourage the pupils to use each word in a sentence. Try to use a pupil's name in every sentence.

Assign Part A.

Introducing Part B

Tell the pupils that in this lesson we will think about the sound /w/ and the blend /hw/. Say them several times and have the pupils do so, also.

Turn to the word list on page 56. Pronounce each word distinctly for the pupils, distinguishing between /hw/ and /w/, and have them pronounce each word after you.

Then give more practice in saying the words correctly by discussing the picture, using a spelling word in each sentence. Here are some examples:

The children are walking.
We can see **where** *they are walking.*
The children are walking in the woods.
Why *are they leaning forward?*
The wind *is blowing.*
The children are wearing warm *clothing.*

Assign Part B on page 57.

Additional Activity:

Write three sentences about the picture at the top of page 56.

In the first sentence, tell who the people are and where they are going.

In the second sentence, tell something else about the boy.

In the third sentence, tell something else about the girl.

Lesson 28

Introducing Part A

While the pupils look at the word list on page 58, say the spelling words and have them say each one after you. Be careful to say /t/, not /d/, in *better.*

For more practice in saying the spelling words, encourage the pupils to use each word in a sentence.

Assign Part A.

Introducing Part B

Direct the pupils to the picture at the top of page 58. Say, "How many mountain peaks do you see in the picture?" *(three)*

Hold your book facing the pupils and point to the first peak, or point to the first peak in several pupils' books, and say, "This peak is *high.* Now you point to the second peak. Is it as high as the first peak? It is *higher* than the first peak.

"Point to the third peak. What could we say about the third peak? Yes, that peak is the *highest* of all of them.

"Spell *high.*

"Spell *higher.*

"Spell *highest."*

Write the three words on the chalkboard. Underline *er* and *est.* Say, "The syllables *e-r* and *e-s-t* are suffixes."

As you together practice saying aloud the list of spelling words, say all three forms of comparison for the third through the seventh words: *big, bigger, biggest; dark, darker, darkest;* and so forth. For the last five, say, *"Much, more, most; good, better, best."*

Assign Part B on page 59.

Lesson 29

Introducing Part A

While the pupils look at the spelling words on page 60, pronounce the words for them and have them say each word after you. See that the pupils end *across* with the /s/ sound and do not add an erroneous /t/ sound to it.

To give more practice in saying the spelling words, help the pupils to use each word in a sentence. As an additional challenge, see if they can use the first two words in one sentence, the next two in another sentence, and so forth.

Assign Part A.

Introducing Part B

Say together the spelling words on page 60.

As the pupils observe the picture at the top of the page, let them tell which spelling words the picture makes them think of.

Write *sell* and *mitten* on the board. Mention that in today's lesson we will think about double consonants. Point out the *ll* in *sell* and the *tt* in *mitten.* Have the class think of more words they know that have double consonants. Write them on the board too. When we learn to spell words, we must watch for double consonants.

Assign Part B on page 61.

Additional Activity:

Write three sentences about the picture at the top of page 60.

In the first sentence, tell about the tree.

In the second sentence, tell about the apples.

In the third sentence, tell how apples can be used.

Lesson 31

Introducing Part A

Pronounce each spelling word on page 64. Have the pupils follow along in the list and say each word after you.

For more practice in saying the words, encourage the pupils to use each word in an oral sentence. To give practice in saying "He doesn't" instead of "He don't," you could ask that each sentence begin with "He doesn't."

Assign Part A.

Introducing Part B

Say together the spelling words on page 64.

"All the spelling words in this lesson name things. Words that name things are called *nouns.* Are these words *singular nouns*—does each word name one thing? Or are these words *plural nouns*—does each word name more than one thing?" *(plural nouns)*

Say the list of words again, this time saying both the singular and plural forms for each word. Ask what letter is added to most singular nouns to spell the plural noun. *(s)* Point out the *es* added to *dish.* Also explain that the singular noun *fly* has a *y,* but the plural noun *flies* has *ies.*

Ask which spelling word is illustrated by the picture at the top of the page. *(stars)*

Assign Part B on page 65.

Additional Activity:

Write three sentences about the picture on page 64.

In the first sentence, tell what time of day it is.

In the second sentence, tell what is shining in the sky.

In the third sentence, tell something else about the stars.

Lesson 32

Introducing Part A

Clearly pronounce each spelling word on page 66 while the pupils look at the word list and say each word after you.

For more practice in saying the words, encourage the pupils to use each word in an oral sentence. Be sure that the suffixes are enunciated when the words are said in sentence context.

Assign Part A.

Introducing Part B

After the pupils turn to the word list on page 66, mention that all these spelling words are verbs. Ask what two suffixes the spelling words end with. *(-ed* and *-ing)*

As you say the spelling words together, first say each word without the suffix and then with the suffix.

Point out the *y* in *carry* and the *ied* in *carried.*

Write the following words on the board.

have	*having*	*save*	*saved*
make	*making*	*bake*	*baked*

Direct the pupils to notice that the final *e* in the root word is dropped to add the suffix.

Can the pupils think up some sentences to tell about the picture at the top of the page? Each sentence should include a spelling word. For example,

The boys *learned* to ride bicycle last week.

The one boy *asked* the other boy if he may ride the bicycle.

Assign Part B on page 67.

Additional Activity:

Write three sentences about the picture at the top of page 66.

In the first sentence, tell something about the one boy.

In the second sentence, tell something about the other boy.

In the third sentence, tell something else about the picture.

Lesson 33

Introducing Part A

Have the pupils look at the word list on page 68 while you pronounce the spelling words for them. Have them say each word after you.

Give more practice in saying the words by helping the pupils to use each word in an oral sentence.

Assign Part A.

Introducing Part B

Saying and spelling words by syllables is especially helpful in spelling words correctly. Write the following words on the chalkboard. Pronounce each one for the pupils. As you say each word, let your finger tap your desk or the chalkboard once at the exact same time that you say the word.

puts	*my*	*green*	*rained*
kite	*hung*	*frog*	*round*

Next repeat the exercise, having the pupils say the words with you and tap their desks at the same time that you tap.

Then write this next set of words on the board. As you say each word for the pupils, let your finger tap your desk twice—once with each syllable. Remember to accent the accented syllable just as you would in normal speaking.

filling	*doctors*	*candy*
quickly	*doorway*	*boxes*

Then repeat the exercise, having the pupils say the words with you and tap their desks at the same time you tap. This helps the pupils to hear and feel the syllables.

Have the pupils turn to page 68 and observe the picture. What spelling words does the picture make them think of? *(water, pony, river)*

This time when you say the spelling words aloud with the pupils, both you and they should tap once with each syllable.

Assign Part B on page 69.

Additional Activity:

Write three sentences about the picture at the top of page 68.

In the first sentence, tell what the animal is and what it is doing.

In the second sentence, tell something about the water.

In the third sentence, tell how the animal will soon feel.

BIBLIOGRAPHY

Anderson, Paul S. *Resource Materials for Teachers of Spelling.* Minneapolis: Burgess Publishing Co., 1959.

Buckingham, B. R., and Dolch, E. W. *A Combined Word List.* Boston: Ginn and Co., 1936.

Carrell, James, and Tiffany, William R. *Phonetics: Theory and Application to Speech Improvement.* New York: McGraw Hill Book Company, 1960.

Ernst, Margaret S. *Words.* New York: Alfred A. Knopf, 1937.

Fitzgerald, James A. *A Basic Life Spelling Vocabulary.* Milwaukee: Bruce Publishing Co., 1951.

Gates, Arthur I. *A List of Spelling Difficulties in 3876 Words.* New York: Bureau of Publications, Teachers College, Columbia University, 1937.

Greene, Harry A. *The New Iowa Spelling Scale.* Iowa City: State University of Iowa, 1954.

Hanna, Paul R.; Hodges, Richard E.; Hanna, Jean S. *Spelling: Structure and Strategies.* Boston: Houghton Mifflin Co., 1971.

Hanna, Paul R.; Hodges, Richard E.; Hanna, Jean S.; and Rudorf, Edwin H., Jr. *Phoneme-Grapheme Correspondences as Cues to Spelling Improvement.* Washington: U.S. Department of Health, Education, and Welfare, 1966.

Hildreth, Gertrude. *Teaching Spelling.* New York: Henry Holt and Co., 1955.

Kurath, Hans. *A Phonology and Prosody of Modern English.* Ann Arbor: University of Michigan Press, 1964.

Peters, Margaret L., and London, Routledge and K. Paul. *Spelling: Caught or Taught?* New York: Humanities Press, 1967.

TEST SENTENCES

(Teacher: To give spelling tests, pronounce each spelling word, read the sentance, and pronounce the word again.)

Lesson 1

1. *big* We saw a *big* white cloud.
2. *fat* Mother roasted the *fat* chicken.
3. *cake* Pie and *cake* are desserts.
4. *rain* God knows when to send *rain* to the earth.
5. *cap* Hang the *cap* on the hook.
6. *days* In six *days* God made the world.
7. *sick* Some children are *sick* for many days.
8. *yes* The opposite of *yes* is no.
9. *hat* Who will bring Father's *hat* to him?
10. *word* We will write one *word* at a time.
11. *ten* The number *ten* is one more than nine.
12. *pig* John feeds the *pig* corn and water.

Lesson 2

1. *can* Lois thinks she *can* help us.
2. *tip* We write with the *tip* of the pencil.
3. *man* The name of the first *man* was Adam.
4. *bell* Who heard the *bell* ring?
5. *yet* Winter has not *yet* come.
6. *his* The man waved *his* hand.
7. *bill* Father paid the *bill* at the store.
8. *top* Twelve is at the *top* of the clock.
9. *cat* The mother *cat* washes her kittens.
10. *doll* Let the girl hold your *doll* again.
11. *nut* The squirrel has a *nut* between his paws.
12. *but* We called, *but* they did not hear.

Lesson 3

1. *map* We keep a road *map* in the car.
2. *net* Jesus told Peter to cast the *net* into the water.
3. *God* The Bible says that *God* is love.
4. *love* We *love* God.
5. *hill* The truck drove up the *hill* slowly.
6. *jar* The buttons in the *jar* are different colors.
7. *keep* Where do you *keep* your boots?
8. *nap* The baby took a long *nap* today.
9. *wet* Everything is *wet* after a rain.
10. *seat* His *seat* is near the window.
11. *mill* The man at the feed *mill* works hard.
12. *met* Father *met* the visitors at the door.

Lesson 4

1. *bus* The driver of the *bus* is careful.
2. *cut* Here is a scissors to *cut* the paper.
3. *did* What *did* he say?
4. *feed* We need more *feed* for the chickens.
5. *road* Cars drive on the *road* every day.
6. *cup* Please give me a *cup* of water.
7. *sat* Mary *sat* and listened to Jesus.
8. *sad* Mary and Martha were *sad* when Lazarus died.
9. *barn* The cows go into the *barn* at night.
10. *feet* Be careful, little *feet,* where you go.
11. *hook* Hang your coat on the *hook,* please.
12. *dig* The men will *dig* a deep ditch.

Lesson 5

1. *train* What a long *train* that was!
2. *from* We read *from* the Bible for devotions.
3. *sweet* Bees make *sweet* honey.
4. *spot* The dog has a black *spot* on his back.
5. *try* Always *try* to do your best.
6. *stop* Where should we *stop* to buy gas?
7. *black* Coal is *black* and shiny.
8. *sleep* Bears *sleep* during the winter.
9. *dry* Use the towel to *dry* your hands.
10. *brown* Most tree trunks are *brown,* aren't they?
11. *drop* A *drop* of water fell onto my hand.
12. *green* In the garden are *green* and yellow beans.

Lesson 6

See page T27.

Lesson 7

1. *head* The cat poked her *head* out the doorway.
2. *ever* Has he *ever* been here?
3. *trap* Mother set a *trap* to catch the mouse.
4. *dead* She threw the *dead* mouse away.
5. *fast* See how *fast* the dogs are running.
6. *left* We *left* home at eight o'clock.
7. *egg* Glenn ate an *egg* for breakfast.
8. *test* We have a *test* every week.
9. *hang* Please *hang* up your clothes.
10. *flag* The red *flag* waved in the wind.
11. *glad* The disciples were *glad* to see Jesus.
12. *said* Jesus *said,* "I am the good shepherd."

Lesson 8

1. *show* Will someone *show* me how to do it?
2. *then* Wait until *then* to go.
3. *shall* "Forgive, and ye *shall* be forgiven.
4. *three* Daniel kneeled *three* times a day to pray.
5. *she* Ruth said *she* would go with Naomi.
6. *cheek* The nut made the squirrel's *cheek* puff out.
7. *this* Is *this* your coat?
8. *thing* The shiny *thing* was a needle.
9. *that* You may open *that* box.
10. *chair* Keep your *chair* legs on the floor.
11. *ship* The people traveled by *ship* on the ocean.
12. *shed* The door of the cattle *shed* was open.

Lesson 9

1. *bunch* We brought a *bunch* of radishes.
2. *both* Roses and raspberries *both* have thorns.
3. *wish* I *wish* I could see her more often.
4. *such* Have you ever tasted *such* sweet berries?
5. *dish* Grandmother gave a *dish* to each girl.
6. *bath* A *bath* in warm water feels good.
7. *push* Try to *push* the swing gently.
8. *brush* Remember to *brush* your hair.
9. *with* A cherry is round *with* a seed in the center.
10. *each* God loves *each* of us.
11. *wash* Naaman was to *wash* in the river.
12. *catch* Peter tried all night to *catch* fish.

Lesson 10

1. *shut* God *shut* the door to the ark.
2. *sun* God created the *sun* on the fourth day.
3. *little* Zacchaeus was a *little* man.
4. *hot* Corn grows in *hot* weather.
5. *bump* The dogs often *bump* into each other.
6. *lift* Can you *lift* the lid?
7. *son* Noah was the *son* of Lamech.
8. *job* Karen's *job* is to sweep the floor.
9. *milk* Drink a glass of *milk* every day.
10. *pond* Deer drink from the *pond* in the evening.
11. *hop* The bunny went *hop, hop* down the path.
12. *front* Someone knocked on the *front* door.

Lesson 11

1. *same* Everyone had the *same* answer.
2. *nose* Raindrops splashed on my *nose* and cheeks.
3. *slide* You may *slide* on the sliding board.
4. *kite* See the big *kite* up in the air.
5. *made* God *made* the earth.
6. *date* The *date* it happened was June 2, 1950.
7. *drive* Father will *drive* the automobile.
8. *home* We will be glad to go *home* again.
9. *dime* A *dime* is worth ten cents.
10. *save* Aunt Mary wants to *save* the stamp.
11. *bake* We *bake* cakes in the oven.
12. *ate* The birds *ate* all the corn.

Lesson 12

See page T28.

Lesson 13

1. *heads* Only their *heads* showed above the tall grass.
2. *beds* Two *beds* are in the bedroom.
3. *girls* Many *girls* like to sew.
4. *birds* Listen to the *birds* sing.
5. *arms* His *arms* were tired from working.
6. *seats* All the *seats* were full.
7. *roads* The map shows which *roads* to drive.
8. *trains* Two *trains* stopped at the station.
9. *trees* Pine *trees* have narrow needles.
10. *boys* Some of the *boys* played tag.
11. *bees* The *bees* make honey for us.
12. *rooms* How many *rooms* are in your house?

Lesson 14

1. *baby* Moses' mother put her *baby* into a basket.
2. *names* The Bible gives many *names* for Jesus.
3. *times* Peter denied Jesus three *times*.
4. *babies* Both *babies* are sleeping.
5. *cows* In the barn are *cows* and chickens.
6. *lines* Are the *lines* straight or crooked?
7. *party* At our *party* we had milk and crackers.
8. *bushes* A row of *bushes* is beside the house.
9. *parties* The girls have *parties* with their dolls.
10. *houses* Some *houses* are made of brick.
11. *nights* For two *nights* they slept away from home.
12. *kisses* When the baby cries, the mother *kisses* him..

Lesson 15

1. *started* We have *started* to take a test.
2. *worked* Noah *worked* hard to build the ark.
3. *talked* Jesus *talked* to the woman at the well.
4. *helped* The Israelite maid *helped* Naaman's wife.
5. *hunted* The shepherd *hunted* for the lost sheep.
6. *washed* The blind man *washed* in the pool of Siloam.
7. *stayed* Samuel *stayed* to help Eli.
8. *missed* Mary and Joseph *missed* Jesus.
9. *turned* They *turned* back to Jerusalem.
10. *snowed* After it *snowed* the ground was white.
11. *rained* How much has it *rained* since yesterday?
12. *played* The children *played* quiet games.

Lesson 16

1. *telling* I heard Mother *telling* him to wait.
2. *falling* Nuts are *falling* from the tree.
3. *putting* Is Gloria *putting* the groceries away?
4. *waiting* He is probably tired of *waiting* for me.
5. *reading* We are *reading* an interesting story.
6. *singing* The birds were *singing* since daybreak.
7. *snowing* When it is *snowing,* we wear boots.
8. *fishing* We saw men *fishing* through the ice.
9. *doing* The boys are *doing* their work.
10. *running* The motor is *running* quietly.
11. *sending* Mother is *sending* two letters today.
12. *saying* The man was *saying* something about fish.

Lesson 17

1. *wood* Cherry *wood* makes pretty furniture.
2. *began* Suddenly the rain *began* to fall.
3. *wagon* James fixed the *wagon* wheel.
4. *eating* The cows are *eating* hay.
5. *hung* We *hung* the pictures on the wall.
6. *father* Jesse was the *father* of David.
7. *Jesus* Cruel men hung *Jesus* on the cross.
8. *Amen* We say *Amen* at the end of our prayers.
9. *mother* Hannah was the *mother* of Samuel.
10. *any* Was there *any* food left?
11. *after* The boy ran *after* the ball.
12. *list* We made a *list* of all the names.

Lesson 18

See page T28.

Lesson 19

1. *away* The robin flew *away* from its nest.
2. *meal* Breakfast is the first *meal* of the day.
3. *table* Come to the *table* for breakfast.
4. *may* Yes, you *may* gather the eggs.
5. *gate* Open the *gate* for the cattle.
6. *key* Turn the *key* to open the lock.
7. *mail* The mailman brings our *mail* to us.
8. *free* Our neighbors gave away *free* puppies.
9. *asleep* Jesus was *asleep* in the boat.
10. *afraid* The disciples were *afraid* in the storm.
11. *money* How much *money* does it cost?
12. *leaf* A sassafras *leaf* sometimes looks like a mitten.

Lesson 20

1. *boat* A small *boat* sailed on the water.
2. *ago* Long *ago* people had no telephones.
3. *find* Try to *find* the answer yourself.
4. *cold* If I am *cold,* I wear a sweater.
5. *buy* Mother will *buy* groceries.
6. *light* A bright *light* shone in the dark.
7. *own* Does each one have his *own* book?
8. *by* A yellow cat sat *by* the door.
9. *fight* Those birds *fight* too much.
10. *blow* The wind might *blow* our papers.
11. *over* The calf jumped *over* the fence.
12. *eye* His right *eye* became blind.

Lesson 21

1. *took* Mother *took* the bread from the oven.
2. *food* The *food* in our lunches is delicious.
3. *pushed* Larry *pushed* the box into the corner.
4. *cook* We will *cook* potatoes for dinner.
5. *moon* The *moon* gets its light from the sun.
6. *shoe* Can you tie your *shoe* yourself?
7. *Jew* Queen Esther was a *Jew.*
8. *looked* Jesus *looked* up to heaven and prayed.
9. *who* Do you know *who* climbed a tree to see Jesus?
10. *full* The bottle is *full* of milk.
11. *shoot* This plant is sending out a new *shoot.*
12. *you* A letter came for *you* in the mail.

Lesson 22

1. *helps* Sunshine *helps* plants to grow.
2. *begins* Spring *begins* here in March.
3. *goes* The robin *goes* north for the summer.
4. *likes* No one *likes* to hear people complain.
5. *gets* The early bird *gets* the worm.
6. *sees* Our cat hides when she *sees* visitors.
7. *needs* Everyone *needs* oxygen to breathe.
8. *plays* That big fish *plays* in the water.
9. *takes* Grandfather *takes* two pills every day.
10. *lives* A Frenchman *lives* in France.
11. *stands* A statue *stands* in the harbor.
12. *turns* The little wheel *turns* the big wheel.

Lesson 23

1. *were* Many butterflies *were* in the air.
2. *herself* She *herself* wrote the poem.
3. *never* In heaven people will *never* be sick.
4. *pearl* The beautiful *pearl* was inside the shell.
5. *paper* Tear the *paper* neatly from the tablet.
6. *yesterday* The day before today we call *yesterday.*
7. *learn* We like to *learn* Bible verses.
8. *words* Try to spell all the *words* correctly.
9. *burn* The priests needed to *burn* sacrifices.
10. *under* Abraham's visitors rested *under* the tree.
11. *first* Genesis is the *first* book in the Bible.
12. *working* Matthew was *working* when Jesus called him.

Lesson 24

See page T28.

Lesson 25

1. *kind* "Be ye *kind* one to another."
2. *coat* Hang up your *coat* and cap.
3. *socks* Mother is mending *socks* today.
4. *ducks* See the many *ducks* in the water.
5. *back* Come *back* again.
6. *seek* Shepherds *seek* their lost sheep.
7. *block* A wooden *block* lay on the floor.
8. *cared* David *cared* for the sheep.
9. *kick* How far can you *kick* the ball?
10. *lakes* There are many *lakes* in Minnesota.
11. *cleaning* Mother is *cleaning* the kitchen.
12. *brick* A loose *brick* fell from the chimney.

Lesson 26

1. *stick* We glue pictures to make them *stick* to the paper.
2. *soft* "A *soft* answer turneth away wrath."
3. *city* The lights in the *city* seem very bright.
4. *sorry* We are *sorry* that you are sick.
5. *nice* Grandmother's flowers look *nice,* don't they?
6. *ice* How thick is the *ice* on the river?
7. *place* I know whose *place* this is.
8. *pass* Please *pass* the butter.
9. *last* The *last* one in should close the door.
10. *talks* Mother *talks* kindly to us.
11. *swing* You may play on the *swing* first.
12. *once* Only *once* did we hear the noise.

Lesson 27

1. *walking* Jesus was *walking* along the road.
2. *while* The disciples listened *while* Jesus spoke.
3. *where* People went to the place *where* Jesus was.
4. *when* We do not know *when* Jesus will come again.
5. *warm* The sunshine feels *warm* on my back.
6. *wake* Did you *wake* during the night?
7. *woods* The trees in the *woods* are wet from the rain.
8. *why* We know *why* the floor is dirty.
9. *win* We like to play games whether we *win* or lose.
10. *wind* See the *wind* blowing the trees.
11. *wild* A tiger is a *wild* animal.
12. *what* Listen to *what* he says.

Lesson 28

1. *larger* Lima beans are *larger* than peas.
2. *bigger* Some cabbage heads are *bigger* than others.
3. *better* Tomatoes like sunshine *better* than shade.
4. *best* Bananas grow *best* in warm climates.
5. *more* Mother bought *more* eggs at the store.
6. *dark* Stars look bright on a *dark* night.
7. *most* The smallest rosebush had the *most* flowers.
8. *much* "Thank you very *much*," he said.
9. *harder* Try *harder* before you give up.
10. *warmer* Afternoons are usually *warmer* than forenoons.
11. *higher* Raise your hand *higher* so that I can see it.
12. *highest* The squirrel climbed to the *highest* branch.

Lesson 29

1. *dinner* Before we eat *dinner,* we wash our hands.
2. *apples* Red and yellow *apples* are in the bowl.
3. *hidden* The mother cat has *hidden* her kittens.
4. *spell* We know how to *spell* many words.
5. *still* Sit *still* and listen.
6. *fell* Big raindrops *fell* from the sky.
7. *add* We can *add* and subtract.
8. *kettle* Mother filled the *kettle* with soup.
9. *off* Take the lid *off* the jar.
10. *called* Robert *called* to his dog.
11. *across* Can you jump *across* the stream?
12. *happy* The children are *happy* to play together.

Lesson 30

See page T28.

Lesson 31

1. *songs* We sang two *songs* first of all.
2. *tests* Our teacher gives *tests* to us.
3. *eyes* He closed his *eyes* and slept.
4. *laws* God gave *laws* to teach us how to live.
5. *yards* The store clerk measured three *yards* of cloth.
6. *cards* We send get-well *cards* to sick people.
7. *doors* All the *doors* are shut.
8. *stores* People shop at the *stores* in town.
9. *flies* Many *flies* buzzed in the air.
10. *stars* I like to look at the *stars* at night.
11. *dishes* Put the clean *dishes* into the cupboard.
12. *wings* Birds use their *wings* to fly.

Lesson 32

1. *asked* God *asked* Job many questions.
2. *carried* Four men *carried* a sick man to Jesus.
3. *liked* David *liked* to tend the sheep.
4. *loving* We try to be *loving* and kind.
5. *passing* The sun is *passing* behind a cloud.
6. *kicked* The horse *kicked* up his heels.
7. *holding* What is he *holding* in his hand?
8. *learned* Have you *learned* your memory verse?
9. *riding* The passengers are *riding* on the train.
10. *owned* Mr. Smith *owned* the house before Mr. Hill did.
11. *burning* The trash is *burning* rapidly.
12. *needed* Mother *needed* sugar from the store.

Lesson 33

1. *storm* There was a great *storm* last week.
2. *into* Noah went *into* the ark.
3. *upon* The sacrifice was laid *upon* the altar.
4. *many* Jesus healed *many* people.
5. *water* Rebekah got *water* for the camels to drink.
6. *hands* I have two *hands* to work for Jesus.
7. *filling* The man is *filling* the oil tank.
8. *river* We crossed the *river* on a bridge.
9. *zoo* At the *zoo* we saw giraffes.
10. *ring* Will the bell *ring* soon?
11. *pony* The *pony* eats grass in the pasture.
12. *carries* The postman *carries* a big bag.

Lesson 34

See page T29.

Lesson 6

1. *yes* We answered *yes* or no.
2. *fat* The farmer has *fat* pigs.
3. *big* I like the *big* red ball.
4. *rain* God sends *rain* to water the earth.
5. *sick* Jesus made *sick* people well.
6. *bell* The cow has a *bell* around her neck.
7. *doll* Mother made my *doll* a new dress.
8. *cat* Give the *cat* some milk.
9. *but* The shirt was torn, *but* Mother mended it.
10. *his* The carpenter did *his* work well.
11. *map* This *map* shows the big rivers.
12. *jar* Our honey *jar* is empty.
13. *hill* The grass on the *hill* is green.
14. *seat* Is anyone's *seat* empty?
15. *God* In the beginning *God* created the world.
16. *cut* Someone should *cut* the cake.
17. *road* That *road* was full of ruts.
18. *sat* The boys *sat* on the bench.
19. *barn* Look for a red *barn* and a white house.
20. *hook* Remember to *hook* the door to keep it shut.
21. *stop* Cars *stop* at *stop* signs.
22. *dry* We stayed *dry* under the big umbrella.
23. *green* The rain made the grass *green* again.
24. *sleep* Did you *sleep* well last night?
25. *spot* The girls played in a grassy *spot.*

Lesson 12

1. *fast* How *fast* the train roared by!
2. *glad* We are *glad* for sunshine.
3. *egg* The hen laid her *egg* in the nest.
4. *head* The cat rubbed her *head* against a post.
5. *said* Someone *said* that it is raining.
6. *then* Father went to the bank and *then* to the mill.
7. *chair* Bring another *chair* to the table. *chair*
8. *ship* The big *ship* sailed on the ocean.
9. *thing* Where does this *thing* belong?
10. *cheek* The teddy bear feels soft against my *cheek.*
11. *wash* Remember to *wash* behind your ears.
12. *catch* Try to *catch* the ball.
13. *bunch* Mother bought a *bunch* of bananas.
14. *dish* Grandmother gave a *dish* to each girl.
15. *both* Bring *both* the bucket and the basket.
16. *little* See the *little* red tomato.
17. *hot* The soup was too *hot* to eat.
18. *sun* The *sun* shone brightly all day.
19. *milk* Here is a glass of *milk* for you.
20. *front* Our visitors come in the *front* door.
21. *save* You can *save* money by not spending it.
22. *drive* We had a pleasant *drive* over the mountain.
23. *home* How good it felt to be *home* again!
24. *made* The widow *made* a cake for Elijah.
25. *kite* A yellow *kite* was caught in the tree.

Lesson 18

1. *boys* May we *boys* have the swings?
2. *girls* Three *girls* walked past the house.
3. *trees* Pine *trees* bear pine cones.
4. *birds* Two *birds* built a nest above the door.
5. *rooms* The *rooms* in their house are big.
6. *nights* In winter the *nights* seem long.
7. *bushes* Look under the *bushes* for the kittens.
8. *houses* All the *houses* looked alike.
9. *babies* Several *babies* cried at once.
10. *cows* At milking time the *cows* walked to the barn.
11. *turned* Father *turned* the steering wheel.
12. *started* Suddenly the wind *started* to blow.
13. *worked* The ants had *worked* hard to build the tunnel.
14. *washed* Have you *washed* your hands?
15. *helped* The boys *helped* Father paint the fence.
16. *singing* Everyone was *singing* happily.
17. *waiting* The sheep are *waiting* to be sheared. *waiting*
18. *falling* I heard something *falling* to the floor.
19. *doing* What are you *doing* now?
20. *running* Why is he *running* so fast?
21. *Jesus* An angel told the shepherds that *Jesus* was born.
22. *mother* Samuel's *mother* made him a coat.
23. *father* "Honour thy *father* and thy mother."
24. *after* The visitors went home *after* dinner.
25. *wagon* The tractor pulled the *wagon* to the field.

Lesson 24

1. *table* Set the *table* for dinner.
2. *away* Father went *away* today.
3. *mail* What came in the *mail* today?
4. *leaf* A maple *leaf* is different from an oak *leaf.*
5. *asleep* The calves are *asleep* in the barn.
6. *find* Can you *find* the leak?
7. *light* The sun gives *light* during the day.
8. *eye* Can you see with one *eye* closed?
9. *boat* John sailed his little *boat* on the water.
10. *blow* You may *blow* out the candle.
11. *you* Mother wants *you* to work now.
12. *moon* Some nights the *moon* shines brightly.
13. *took* The mechanic *took* the wheel off the truck.
14. *shoe* Please tie your left *shoe* again.
15. *full* The dam is *full* of water now.
16. *needs* The baker *needs* more flour.
17. *lives* Grandmother *lives* in a small house.
18. *helps* When everyone *helps,* the work gets done fast.
19. *sees* Jane *sees* the train go by every day.
20. *goes* My shadow always *goes* with me.
21. *under* See the dog *under* the tree.
22. *first* Adam was the *first* man.
23. *working* Samuel was *working* in the temple.
24. *burn* The priests needed to *burn* sacrifices.
25. *learn* We try to *learn* Bible verses.

Lesson 30

1. *back* Come *back* to where you started.
2. *coat* My *coat* has big pockets.
3. *kick* That cow might *kick;* so stay back.
4. *seek* We will *seek* until we find it.
5. *cleaning* The girls are *cleaning* the house today.
6. *soft* How *soft* the rabbit feels!
7. *place* The Keeners' *place* is along this road.
8. *swing* The wind made the sign *swing* back and forth.
9. *pass* Quietly *pass* to your seats.
10. *city* Houses in a *city* are close together.
11. *wild* A lion is a *wild* animal.
12. *what* Do you know *what* I did?
13. *when* We get up *when* Mother calls.
14. *warm* Coats keep us *warm* when it is cold.
15. *where* This is *where* we learn our lesson.
16. *harder* Some lessons are *harder* than others.
17. *better* Ripe peaches taste *better* than green ones.
18. *much* Ask how *much* it costs.
19. *highest* What was the *highest* temperature yesterday?
20. *bigger* We need a *bigger* box.
21. *across* The ferry goes *across* the lake.
22. *dinner* Some visitors at *dinner* with us.
23. *spell* Be sure to *spell* your name right.
24. *apples* The jars are full of *apples* and cherries.
25. *add* We *add* to find the sum.

Lesson 34

1. *stars* How bright the *stars* are shining!
2. *doors* Close all the *doors* and windows.
3. *eyes* The bright light made my *eyes* hurt.
4. *songs* We know many *songs* by memory.
5. *dishes* Wash the *dishes* carefully.
6. *flies* An airplane *flies* high in the sky.
7. *wings* The eagle lifted its *wings* and soared away.
8. *cards* We send get-well *cards* to sick people.
9. *holding* The conductor is *holding* all the tickets.
10. *burning* Father is *burning* trash today.
11. *needed* No one *needed* more time.
12. *asked* Charles *asked* for the green crayon.
13. *riding* We like to go *riding* in the car.
14. *liked* All of us *liked* that story.
15. *carried* The boy *carried* our groceries to the car.
16. *passing* The day is *passing* rapidly.
17. *into* Step *into* your boots.
18. *storm* During the *storm* big trees blew over.
19. *upon* Jesus rode *upon* a donkey.
20. *hands* "Work with your own *hands*" is a Bible verse.
21. *water* We need *water* to wash our clothes.
22. *many* How *many* kinds do you have?
23. *filling* We are *filling* the jugs with milk.
24. *carries* The postman *carries* the mail.
25. *river* Water flooded the *river* bank.

Final Test

1. *rain* See how fast the *rain* is falling.
2. *his* The man ate *his* lunch under the tree.
3. *hill* Climbing the steep *hill* made us puff.
4. *road* Beside the *road* were some pretty flowers.
5. *sleep* Children need many hours of *sleep* at night.
6. *head* Bring in a *head* of lettuce.
7. *thing* What is that *thing* on the ceiling?
8. *catch* I could hardly *catch* the ball.
9. *milk* People use *milk* to make cheese.
10. *made* Mother *made* four pies.
11. *mail* We send *mail* at the post office.
12. *eye* Close your right *eye* a bit.
13. *shoe* Did you find your other *shoe* yet?
14. *helps* This salve *helps* to stop the itching.
15. *first* Sweep the floor *first* of all.
16. *back* "Come *back* again," they said.
17. *place* You may *place* your things on the table. *place*
18. *when* Read clearly *when* your turn comes.
19. *highest* What was the *highest* temperature yesterday?
20. *apples* These red *apples* are delicious.
21. *dishes* I will wash the *dishes* now.
22. *asked* God *asked* Job many questions.
23. *water* The *water* in the lake looked blue.
24. *worked* He sang as he *worked* all day.
25. *singing* The boys and girls are *singing* happily.

WORD LIST

This alphabetical list includes all the words taught in the spelling word lists in this book. The numeral after each word indicates the lesson in which the word is taught. In addition to learning these words, the pupils learn to spell many related words in the exercises.

A

across 29
add 29
afraid 19
after 17
ago 20
Amen 17
any 17
apples 29
arms 13
asked 32
asleep 19
ate 11
away 19

B

babies 14
baby 14
back 25
bake 11
barn 4
bath 9
beds 13
bees 13
began 17
begins 22
bell 2
best 28
better 28
big 1
bigger 28
bill 2
birds 13
black 5
block 25
blow 20
boat 20
both 9
boys 13
brick 25
brown 5
brush 9
bump 10
bunch 9
burn 23
burning 32
bus 4
bushes 14
but 2
buy 20
by 20

C

cake 1
called 29
can 2
cap 1
cards 31
cared 25
carried 32
carries 33
cat 2
catch 9
chair 8
cheek 8
city 26
cleaning 25
coat 25
cold 20
cook 21
cows 14
cup 4
cut 4

D

dark 28
date 11
days 1
dead 7
did 4
dig 4
dime 11
dinner 29
dish 9
dishes 31
doing 16
doll 2
doors 31
drive 11
drop 5
dry 5
ducks 25

E

each 9
eating 17
egg 7
ever 7
eye 20
eyes 31

F

falling 16
fast 7
fat 1
father 17
feed 4
feet 4
fell 29
fight 20
filling 33
find 20
first 23
fishing 16
flag 7
flies 31
food 21
free 19
from 5
front 10
full 21

G

gate 19
gets 22
girls 13
glad 7
God 3
goes 22
green 5

H

hands 33
hang 7
happy 29
harder 28
hat 1
head 7
heads 13
helped 15
helps 22
herself 23
hidden 29
higher 28
highest 28
hill 3
his 2
holding 32
home 11
hook 4
hop 10
hot 10
houses 14
hung 17
hunted 15

I

ice 26
into 33

J

jar 3
Jesus 17
Jew 21
job 10

K

keep 3
kettle 29
key 19
kick 25
kicked 32
kind 25
kisses 14
kite 11

L

lakes 25
larger 28
last 26
laws 31
leaf 19
learn 23
learned 32
left 7
lift 10
light 20
liked 32
likes 22
lines 14
list 17
little 10
lives 22
looked 21
love 3
loving 32

M

made 11
mail 19
man 2
many 33
map 3
may 19
meal 19
met 3
milk 10
mill 3
missed 15
money 19
moon 21
more 28
most 28
mother 17
much 28

N

names 14
nap 3
needed 32
needs 22
net 3
never 23
nice 26
nights 14
nose 11
nut 2

O

off 29
once 26
over 20
own 20
owned 32

P

paper 23
parties 14
party 14
pass 26
passing 32
pearl 23
pig 1
place 26
played 15
plays 22
pond 10
pony 33
push 9
pushed 21
putting 16

R

rain 1
rained 15
reading 16
riding 32
ring 33
river 33
road 4
roads 13
rooms 13
running 16

S

sad 4
said 7
same 11
sat 4
save 11
saying 16
seat 3
seats 13
seek 25
sees 22
sending 16
shall 8
she 8
shed 8
ship 8
shoe 21
shoot 21
show 8
shut 10
sick 1
singing 16
sleep 5
slide 11
snowed 15
snowing 16
socks 25
soft 26
son 10
songs 31
sorry 26
spell 29
spot 5
stands 22
stars 31
started 15
stayed 15
stick 26
still 29
stop 5
stores 31
storm 33
such 9
sun 10
sweet 5
swing 26

T

table 19
takes 22
talked 15
talks 26
telling 16
ten 1
test 7
tests 31
that 8
then 8
thing 8
this 8
three 8
times 14
tip 2
took 21
top 2
train 5
trains 13
trap 7
trees 13
try 5
turned 15
turns 22

U

under 23
upon 33

W

wagon 17
waiting 16
wake 27
walking 27
warm 27
warmer 28
wash 9
washed 15
water 33
were 23
wet 3
what 27
when 27
where 27
while 27
who 21
why 27
wild 27
win 27
wind 27
wings 31
wish 9
with 9
wood 17
woods 27
word 1
words 23
worked 15
working 23

Y

yards 31
yes 1
yesterday 23
yet 2
you 21

Z

zoo 33

For Christian Schools

SPELLING

By Sound and Structure

2

Rod and Staff Publishers, Inc.
P.O. Box 3, Hwy. 172
Crockett, Kentucky 41413
Telephone: 606-522-4348

Acknowledgments

We acknowledge the everlasting God, the Lord, beside whom there is none else. His blessing made the writing and publishing of this book possible.

To the following persons, we express gratitude: the writer, Rachel K. Weaver; the editor, Marvin Eicher; the reviewers, Julia Torkelson, Joan Wenger, Isaac Martin, and Loyal Troyer. For the illustrating, appreciation is given to Edith Burkholder.

We are indebted to numerous people who assisted in the work by helping in related projects along the way, by providing finances, by encouraging those working most directly with it, and by interceding in prayer for the work.

We are grateful to the writers and publishers of the materials we consulted for reference in preparing this book—various word lists, reports on research, instruction in teaching spelling, and other spelling series.

—The Publishers

Printed in U.S.A.

ISBN 978-07399-0571-5
Catalog no. 16221

17 18 19 20 21 — 21 20 19 18 17 16 15 14 13 12

ISBN 978-07399-0572-2
Catalog no. 16291

14 15 16 17 18 — 21 20 19 18 17 16 15 14 13 12

Table of Contents

LESSON 1

See Introductions, page T11;
Test Sentences, page T23.

Purpose
To teach the pupil to hear the first sound in a word, and to teach how to spell consonant sounds at the beginning of words.

cap
ten
days
word
rain
big
hat
sick
fat
yes
cake
pig

PART A

Write spelling words in the blanks.

1. It has four legs.
2. It falls from the sky.
3. It is good to eat.
4. It is one more than nine.
5. There are seven of these in one week.
6. It means the opposite of **no.**

1. pig
2. rain
3. cake
4. ten
5. days
6. yes

7. Read this sentence.

The boy wears a ——— on his head.

We could put spelling words in the sentence.

The boy wears a **cap** on his head.
The boy wears a **hat** on his head.

What spelling words could fit in this sentence?

We saw a ——— dog.

big sick fat

PART B

1. Say the names of these pictures. Listen for the first sound in each word.

ball  bed 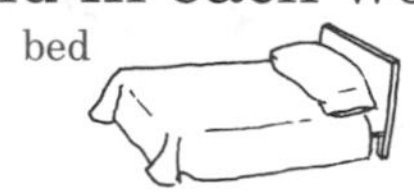

Which spelling word begins with the same sound that begins ball and bed?

The letter **b** spells the first sound.

2. Say the name of each picture.

Write the spelling word that begins with the same sound. On the short line write the letter that spells the first sound.

dog  days 

fish  fat 

hand  hat 

pie  pig 

rooster  rain 

sun  sick s

turtle  ten 

wagon  word 

yarn yes 

3. Write the spelling words that name these pictures.

cap  cake

cap cake

What letter spells the first sound?

c

4. Write **ten.** Then write other words by changing the first letter to **m, p,** and **h.**

ten pen

men hen

LESSON 2

See Introductions, page T11;
Test Sentences, page T23.

Purpose
To teach the pupil to hear the second sound in a word, and to teach common spellings of short vowel sounds.

top
can
bell
nut
tip
man
but
yet
doll
cat
bill
his

PART A

Write spelling words in the blanks.

1. It has a shell on the outside.
2. The teacher rings this.
3. A bird uses this to get his food.
4. You write with this part of the pencil.
5. We can buy paint in this at the store.
6. It means the opposite of **bottom.**

1. nut
2. bell
3. bill
4. tip
5. can
6. top

7. Which spelling word fits in this sentence?

Joseph feeds ——— dog every day.

his

8. What spelling words could fit in this sentence?

The ——— has two shining eyes.

man doll cat

PART B

1. Listen to the first sound in apple. Listen to the second sound in cap. The second sound in cap is like the first sound in apple. What letter spells this sound?

a

2. What spelling words have the same second sound as cap has?

can cat

man

3. Say the name of each picture. Listen to the second sound. Write the spelling words that have the same second sound. In the short blank write the letter that spells the second sound.

fish

tip i

bill i

his i

bed

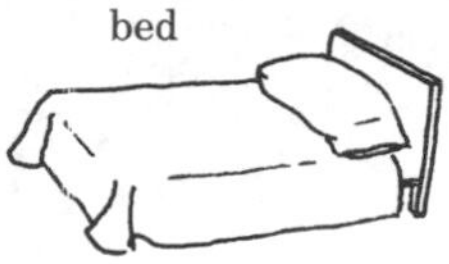

bell e

yet e

fox

top o

doll o

cup

nut u

but u

4. Write **but** and **mud.** Then write other words by changing the second letter in each word to **a.**

but bat

mud mad

LESSON 3

See Introductions, page T12;
Test Sentences, page T23.

Purpose
To give more practice in hearing and spelling the first sound in a word.

God
keep
map
nap
met
net
love
hill
jar
wet
mill
seat

PART A

Write spelling words in the blanks.

1. He made the earth.
2. This is how water feels.
3. It is made for people to sit on.
4. Some men use this to catch fish.
5. You could carry milk in this.
6. This is what we call a short sleep.

1. God
2. wet
3. seat
4. net
5. jar
6. nap

Which spelling words fit in these sentences?

7. We ——— God most of all.
8. The man at the ——— grinds wheat.
9. A ——— shows where the roads are.
10. Mother ——— us at the door when we came home.

7. love
8. mill
9. map
10. met

PART B

1. Say the names of these pictures. Listen for the first sound in each word.

Which spelling words begin with the same sound that begins [nest] and [nail]?

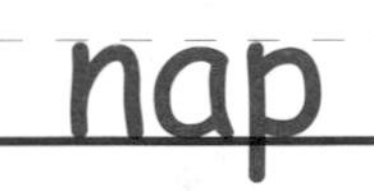
nap

net

What letter spells the first sound?

n

2. Say the name of each picture.

Write a spelling word that begins with the same sound. In the short blank write the letter that spells the first sound.

hill

h

God

G or g

jar

j

seat

s

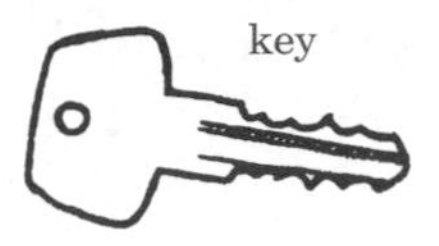

keep

k

love

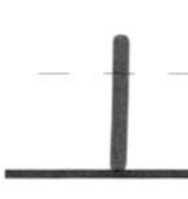
l

wet

w

3. Write **wet.** Then write other words by changing the first letter to **l, s,** and **p.**

wet

set

let

pet

4. Write **mill.** Then write other words by changing the first letter to **f, t, k, d,** and **p.**

mill

kill

fill

dill

till

pill

LESSON 4

See Introductions page T12;
Test Sentences page T23.

Purpose
To teach the pupil to hear the last sound in a word, and to teach how to spell consonant sounds at the end of words.

road
barn
bus
feed
feet
did
dig
cup
cut
sad
sat
hook

PART A

1. We use a 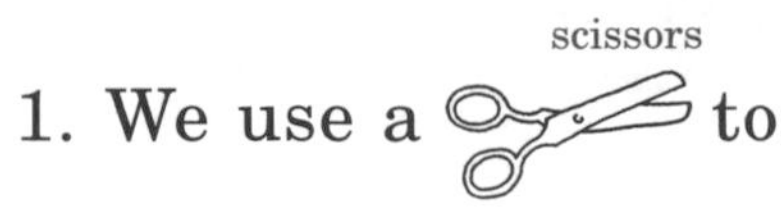 (scissors) to cut.

2. We use a  (shovel) to dig.

3. (cars) drive on a road.

4. (horses) and (cows) eat feed.

5. We wear  (shoes) on our feet.

6. We keep  (animals) in a barn.

7. Many (people) can ride on a bus.

8. We drink (water) from a cup.

PART B

1. Listen to the first sound in door. Listen to the last sound in cloud. The last sound in cloud is like the first sound in door. What letter spells this sound?

d

2. What spelling words have the same last sound as cloud has?

road did

feed sad

3. Say the name of each picture. Listen to the last sound. Write the spelling words that have the same last sound. In the short blank write the letter that spells the last sound.

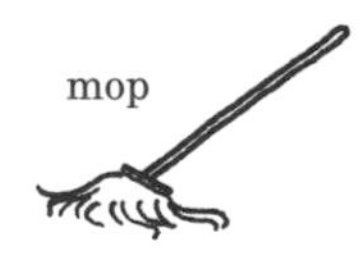

mop

cup  p

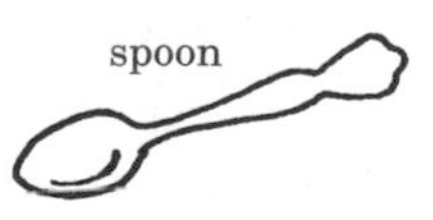

spoon

barn n

book

hook k

grass

bus s

goat

feet t

cut t

sat t

4. Write the spelling words that begin with these letters. Circle the last letter in every word you write.

sa— sad sat

di— dig did

cu— cup cut

5. Write **barn.** Then write another word by changing the last letter to **k.**

barn bark

See Introductions, page T12;
Test Sentences, page T23.

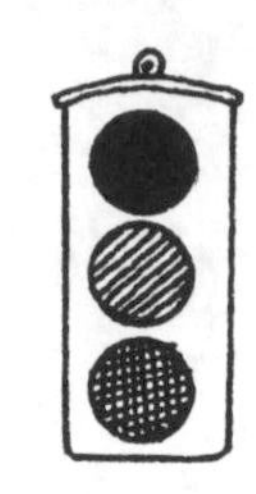

Purpose
To teach how to spell consonant blends at the beginning of words.

sleep
spot
train
black
brown
from
green
drop
sweet
dry
try
stop

PART A

Write spelling words in the blanks.

1. What runs on a track?
2. What do you do at night?
3. How do oranges taste?
4. How does dust feel?
5. What means the same as **fall?**
6. What is the opposite of **go?**

1. train
2. sleep
3. sweet
4. dry
5. drop
6. stop

Which spelling words fit in these sentences?

7. Please ——— to open this jar.
8. Bread is made ——— flour.

7. try
8. from

9. What spelling words name colors and could fit in this sentence?

The girl has a ——— coat.

black brown green

PART B

1. Say the names of these pictures. Listen for the first two sounds in each word. tree truck

Which spelling words begin with the same sounds that begin and ?

train try

What two letters spell the first sounds?

tr

A **consonant blend** is two or more consonant sounds very close together.

2. Name each picture. Listen for the beginning consonant blend. Write a spelling word that begins with the same blend. Then write the two letters that spell the beginning blend.

black bl

brown br

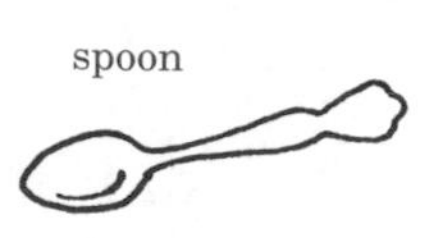

spot sp

from fr

grass

green gr

sweet sw

sleep sl

drop dr

dry dr

3. Write **drop, grand,** and **pray.** Then write other words by changing the beginning blends to **st.**

drop stop

grand stand

pray stay

Purpose
To review concepts taught in Lessons 1–5.

No new concepts are introduced. Pupils can begin right away to do the exercises.

If a pupil's work in any exercise is poor, refer to the lesson in which the concept was taught. Reteach and give more practice.

See suggested test words and sentences, page T27.

1	2	3	4	5
cap	top	God	road	sleep
ten	can	keep	barn	spot
days	bell	map	bus	train
word	nut	nap	feed	black
rain	tip	met	feet	brown
big	man	net	did	from
hat	but	love	dig	green
sick	yet	hill	cup	drop
fat	doll	jar	cut	sweet
yes	cat	wet	sad	dry
cake	bill	mill	sat	try
pig	his	seat	hook	stop

PART A REVIEW

Fill in the puzzle with words from Lessons 1–5 that have these meanings. Print one letter in each block.

Pupils should print puzzle answers in all capital letters.

1. A short sleep
2. Something that rings
3. Tasting like sugar or honey
4. A building for animals
5. Belonging to him
6. Three more than seven
7. A place to sit
8. Railroad cars connected together
9. The parts at the ends of people's legs
10. Turn ground over

PART B REVIEW

1. Say the names of the pictures. Listen for the beginning sounds. Write the words from Lessons 1–5 that begin with the same sounds.

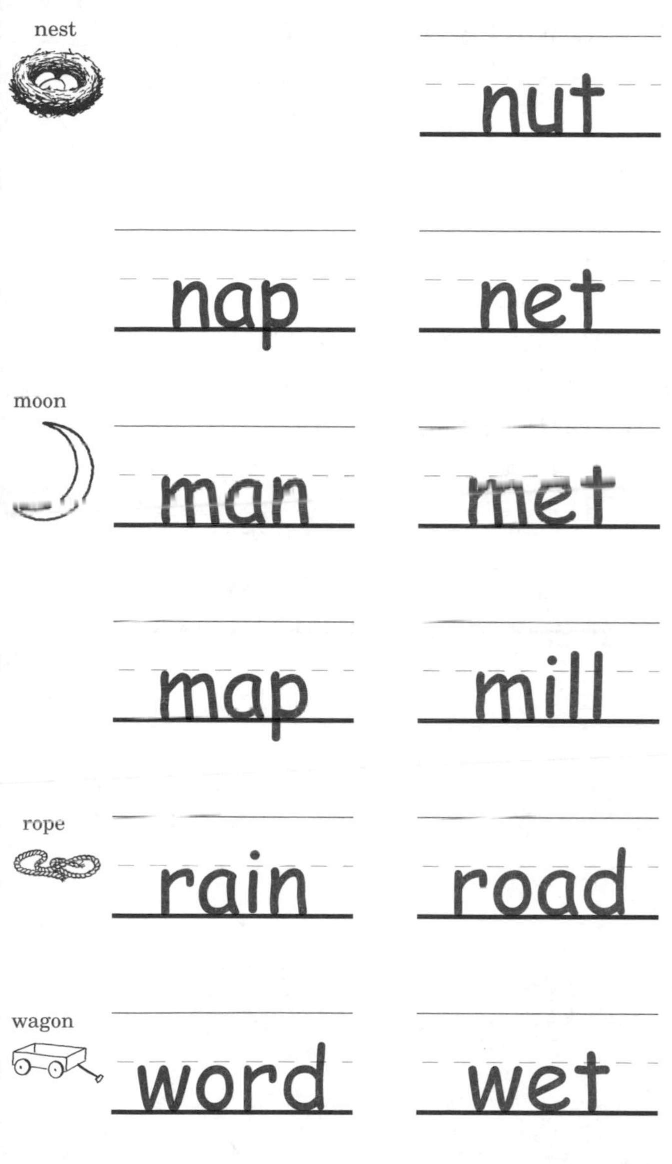

2. Write the Lesson 4 word that names this picture. cup Which Lesson 1 word ends with the same sound?

3. Which Lesson 1 words end with **g**?

big pig

4. Listen for the second sounds. Write the words after the pictures that have the same second sounds.

sick yes can bus God

hand — can

bed — yes

fish — sick

fox — God

duck — bus

5. Which Lesson 5 words begin with these blends?

sp gr fr bl

spot from

green black

See Introductions, page T13; Test Sentence page T23.

m_n

Purpose
To teach common spellings of /a/ and /e/.

fast
flag
ever
test
glad
head
left
trap
hang
egg
dead
said

PART A

Write spelling words in the blanks.

1. It is good to eat.
2. Pictures do this on the wall.
3. We use this to catch mice.
4. You feel like this when you are happy.
5. It tells how we move when we hurry.
6. This word means "did speak."
7. Your face is the front part of this.
8. Your heart is on this side of your body.
9. This is usually made of cloth.
10. It is the opposite of **alive.**

1. egg
2. hang
3. trap
4. glad
5. fast
6. said
7. head
8. left
9. flag
10. dead

PART B

1. Listen to the first sound in apple. Listen to the second sound in hat.

The letter **a** spells this short vowel sound. Circle **a** in these words.

apple **hat**

2. Which spelling words have the same short vowel sound that you hear in apple and hat?

fast trap

flag hang

glad

3. Write **song, on,** and **is.** Then write other words by changing the vowels to **a.**

song sang

on an

is as

4. Write the spelling word that names this picture. egg

egg

Listen to the first sound in egg. Listen to the second sound in bell.

The letter **e** spells this short vowel sound. Circle **e** in these words.

egg **bell**

5. Name these pictures. bread thread

Sometimes the short **e** sound is spelled **ea.** Circle **ea** in these words.

bread **thread**

6. Which spelling words have the short **e** sound spelled **e** like in **bell**?

ever left

test egg

7. Which spelling words have the short **e** sound spelled **ea** like in **bread?**

head dead

8. Write **said.**

said

The short **e** sound is spelled **ai.** Write **said** again and circle **ai.**

said

LESSON 8

See Introductions, page T13;
Test Sentences, page T24.

__ip

Purpose
To teach the pupils to hear the digraphs /ch/, /sh/, /th/, and /th/ at the beginning of words, and to teach their common spellings.

cheek
chair
shed
show
she
ship
shall
thing
three
then
this
that

PART A

Write spelling words in the blanks.
1. What sails on the sea?
2. What do we sit on?
3. What is one part of a person's face?
4. How many is two less than five?
5. Which word names a kind of building?
6. Which word can you say instead of a girl's name?

1. ship 4. three

2. chair 5. shed

3. cheek 6. she

7. What spelling words could fit in this sentence?
Take ——— box to Grandmother.

this that

Which spelling words fit in these sentences?
8. Please ——— me your paper.
9. First comes winter, ——— spring.

8. show 9. then

PART B

1. Say the names of these pictures. Listen for the first sound in every name.

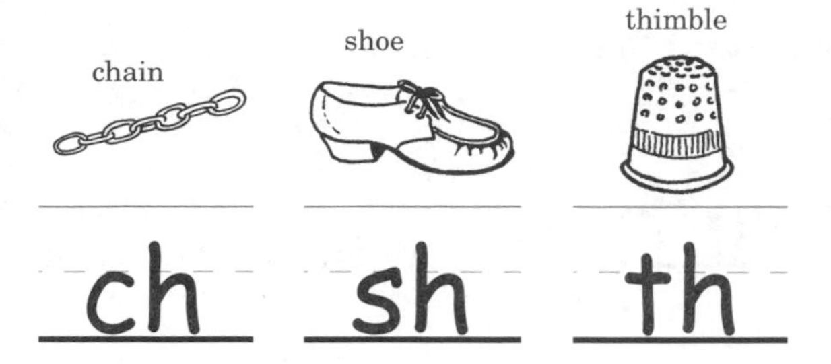

ch sh th

These first sounds are spelled with two letters. Under the pictures write **ch, sh,** and **th.**

2. Which spelling words begin with the same sound that begins ?

cheek chair

What two letters spell the first sound?

ch

3. Which spelling words begin with the same sound that begins ?

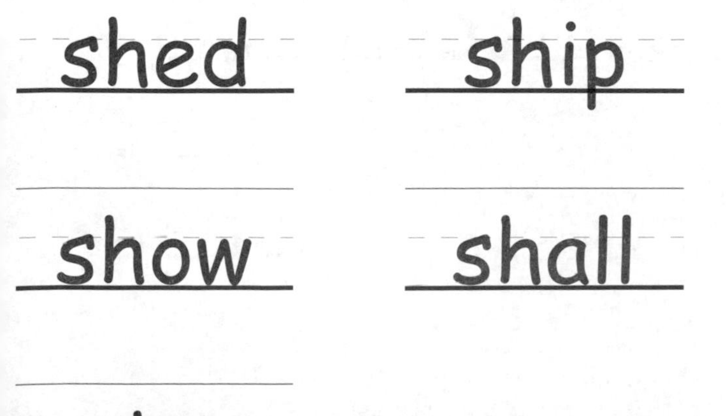

shed ship

show shall

she

What two letters spell the first sound?

sh

4. Two spelling words begin with the same sound that begins .
Write **thing** and **three.**

thing three

5. Listen to the first sound in these words. **those them there**
Three spelling words begin with this same first sound. Write **then, this,** and **that.**

then that

this

6. Take away the first letter in these words. Write other words that begin with **sh. dot pout lift rock**

shot shift

shout shock

7. Write **she** and **the.**

she the

LESSON 9

See Introductions, page T13;
Test Sentences, page T24.

Purpose
To teach pupils to hear the digraphs /ch/, /sh/, and /th/ at the end of words, and to teach their common spellings.

dish
brush
bunch
each
wash
both
bath
catch
wish
push
with
such

PART A

1. I brush my teeth with a toothbrush.

2. Pull the wagon when I push.

3. Try to catch the ball.

4. Wash your dirty hands.

5. I use soap to take a bath.

6. God makes each pretty cloud.

7. bananas are in the red dish.

8. Use a pencil with a sharp point.

PART B

1. Hear the first sound in (shoe). Hear the last sound in (fish). Write the spelling words that end like (fish) ends.

dish wish

brush push

wash

What two letters spell this sound?

sh

2. Take away the last letter in each of these words. Write other words that end with **sh.** **sad** **fit** **mug** **trap**

sash mush

fish trash

3. Hear the first sound in (chain). Hear the last sound in (peach). Which spelling words end with the same sound that ends (peach)?

bunch each

catch such

Which word you wrote ends with **tch**?

catch

In the other three words, the two letters ch spell the last sound.

4. Hear the first sound in (thimble). Hear the last sound in (teeth *or* mouth). Write the spelling words that end like (teeth) ends.

both

bath with

The two letters th spell this sound.

5. Take away the last letter in each of these words. Write other words that end with **th.** **pan** **earn**

path earth

See Introductions, page T14;
Test Sentences, page T24.

Purpose
To teach common spellings of /i/, /o/, and /u/.

shut
bump
little
front
hop
hot
lift
sun
son
milk
pond
job

PART A

1. Rabbits do this.
2. It shines in the sky.
3. Cows and goats give this.
4. This is made of water.
5. This is what a father calls his boy.
6. It means "to pick something up or to make higher."
7. It means the opposite of **big.**
8. It means the opposite of **open.**
9. It means the opposite of **cold.**
10. It means the opposite of **back.**

1. hop
2. sun
3. milk
4. pond
5. son
6. lift
7. little
8. shut
9. hot
10. front

PART B

1. Listen to the first sound in igloo.
Listen to the second sound in pig.
The letter **i** spells this short vowel sound. Circle **i** in these words.

(i)gloo **p(i)g**

2. Which spelling words have the same short vowel sound that you hear in igloo and pig?

little

lift milk

3. What words can you make by changing the vowels in **fat** and **hem** to **i?**

fit him

4. Listen to the second sound in box and mop. The letter **o** spells this short vowel sound. Circle **o** in these words. **b(o)x** **m(o)p**

5. Which spelling words have the same short vowel sound that you hear in box and mop?

hop pond

hot job

6. What words can you make by changing the vowels in **rack** and **pep** to **o**?

rock pop

7. Listen to the second sound in cup and duck. The letter **u** spells this short vowel sound. Circle **u** in these words. **c(u)p** **d(u)ck**

8. Say these spelling words that have the short **u** sound like in cup.

shut bump front sun son

Which of those words have the vowel sound spelled **u**?

shut sun

bump

Which of those words have the vowel sound spelled **o**?

front son

9. What words can you make by changing the vowels in **tab** and **trick** to **u**?

tub truck

See Introductions, page T14;
Test Sentences, page T24.

Purpose
To teach long vowel spellings in words that end with vowel-consonant-*e*.

bake
dime
drive
made
slide
home
save
ate
date
kite
nose
same

PART A

1. This is part of your face.
2. This is where people live.
3. Feet do this on ice.
4. It is a piece of money.
5. It flies in the wind.
6. Cars do this on the road.

1. nose 4. dime

2. home 5. kite

3. slide 6. drive

7. What spelling words could fit in this sentence?

Lois ——— a good dinner.

made ate

Which spelling words have these meanings?

8. "Alike; not different"
9. "Cook in an oven"

8. same 9. bake

PART B

1. Say the names of these pictures. Hear the long vowel sounds.

gate knife bone

In every picture name, the long vowel sound is the next-to-last sound.

gate **knife** **bone**

Which picture name ends with

the **f** sound? knife

the **n** sound? bone

the **t** sound? gate

What letter ends every picture name?

e

2. In many words the letter **e** at the end helps to spell the long vowel sound. Which spelling words have the long **a** sound coming next to last, as in **gate**?

bake save

made ate

date same

3. Which spelling words have the long **i** sound coming next to last, as in **knife**?

dime slide

drive kite

4. Which spelling words have the long **o** sound coming next to last, as in **bone**?

home nose

5. What letter at the end of every spelling word helps to spell the long vowel sound?

e

6. Write **lake** and **tame.** Then write other words by changing **a** to **i.**

lake like

tame time

Purpose
To review concepts taught in Lessons 7–11.

If a pupil's work in any exercise is poor, refer to the lesson in which the concept was taught. Reteach and give more practice.

No new concepts are introduced. Pupils can begin right away to do the exercises.

See suggested test words and sentences, page T28.

7	8	9	10	11
fast	cheek	dish	shut	bake
flag	chair	brush	bump	dime
ever	shed	bunch	little	drive
test	show	each	front	made
glad	she	wash	hop	slide
head	ship	both	hot	home
left	shall	bath	lift	save
trap	thing	catch	sun	ate
hang	three	wish	son	date
egg	then	push	milk	kite
dead	this	with	pond	nose
said	that	such	job	same

PART A REVIEW

Fill in the puzzle with words from Lessons 7–11 that have these meanings. Print one letter in each block.

Pupils should print puzzle answers in all capital letters.

1. A quick short jump
2. Not living anymore
3. A seat to sit on
4. Ten cents
5. Very warm
6. A bright light in the daytime sky
7. Happy
8. Two more than one
9. The place a person lives
10. Took into the mouth and swallowed

PART B REVIEW

1. Say these words and name the pictures. Listen for the short vowel sounds. Write the words beside the pictures that have the same vowel sounds.

pond **shall** **milk**

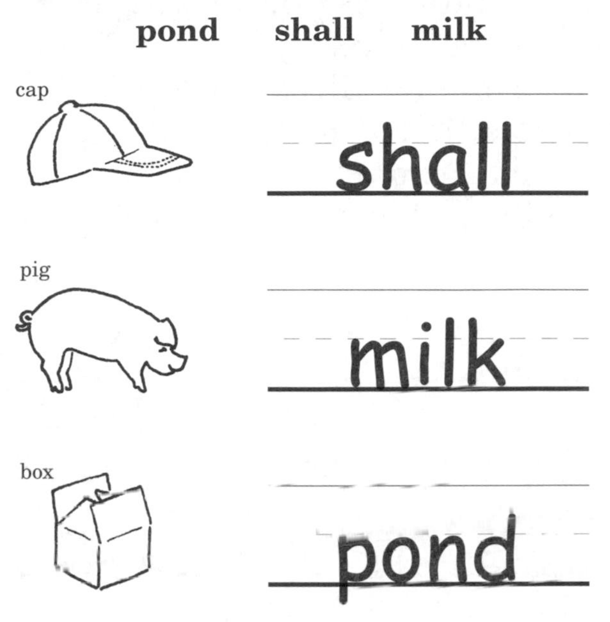

cap shall

pig milk

box pond

2. Hear the short vowel sound in egg. Write **left, head,** and **said.** Tell which letters spell the vowel sound.

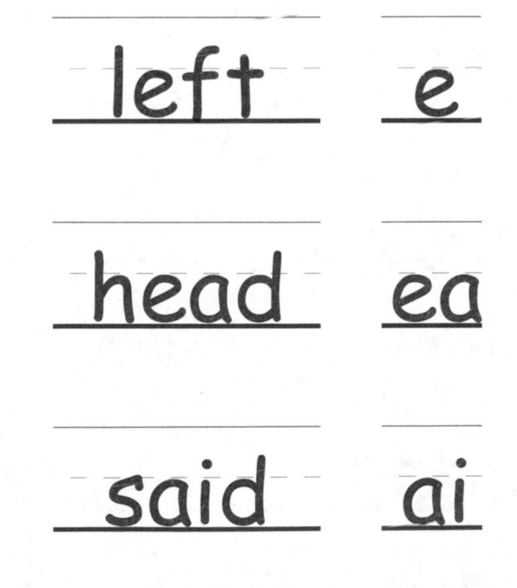

left e

head ea

said ai

3. Hear the short vowel sound in truck. Write **such** and **front.** Tell which letters spell the short vowel sound.

such u

front o

4. What letter at the end of every Lesson 11 word helps to spell the long vowel sound? e

Write **bake, drive, nose,** and **kite.**

bake nose

drive kite

5. Listen for the last sounds. Write the words beside the pictures that have the same last sounds.

both **wash** **catch**

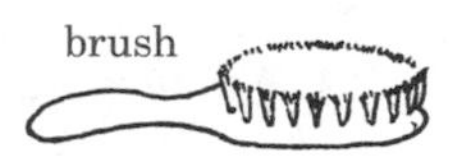

wash

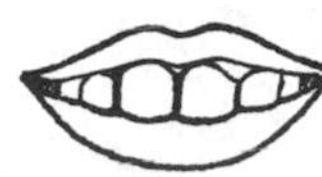

both

peach catch

LESSON 13

See Introductions, page T15;
Test Sentences, page T24.

Purpose
To teach how to form plural nouns by adding *-s*.

roads
seats
trains
arms
trees
birds
boys
girls
bees
heads
rooms
beds

PART A

1. What do cars and trucks drive on?
2. What plants have leaves and trunks?
3. What things run on railroad tracks?
4. What do people lie on to sleep?
5. What do people sit on?
6. Inside a building, what do the walls separate?

1. roads
2. trees
3. trains
4. beds
5. seats
6. rooms

7. What spelling words could fit in these sentences?

The ——— said they are ready to work.

boys girls

See the ——— flying in the air.

birds bees

PART B

1. The word **bee** means "one insect that makes honey." What spelling word means "more than one insect that makes honey"?

bees

2. Write **boy, boys, girl,** and **girls** below the correct pictures.

boy

boys

girl

girls

3. What letter can be added to a word to make it mean more than one?

s

4. Write **arm, head,** and **road.** Then add **s** to make words that mean more than one **arm, head,** and **road.**

arm | arms

head | heads

road | roads

5. Write the names of these pictures.

tree

trees

bird

birds

bed

beds

train

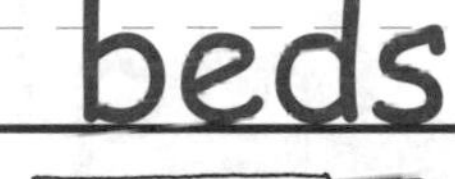

trains

6. The word **plural** means "more than one of something." Write **toy, seat,** and **room.** Then write their plurals.

toy | toys

seat | seats

room | rooms

7. What letter is added to many words to make them plural?

s

LESSON 14

See Introductions, page T15;
Test Sentences, page T24.

Purpose
To give more practice in forming plural nouns by adding *-s*, and to teach how to form plural nouns by adding *-es*.

names
times
nights
cows
lines
bushes
houses
kisses
baby
babies
party
parties

PART A

1. We call people by their ——.
2. It rained for forty days and ——.
3. Carpenters build ——.
4. Bird nests are hidden in the ——.
5. Horses and —— are in the pasture.
6. Draw two straight —— on your paper.
7. Sara read the story two ——.
8. I gave the baby two —— on his cheek.
9. We are having a —— under the tree.
10. We like to have —— under the big tree.

1. names
2. nights
3. houses
4. bushes
5. cows
6. lines
7. times
8. kisses
9. party
10. parties

PART B

1. The word **cow** means one animal. Write **cow.** Then write the spelling word that means more than one cow.

cow cows

2. Words that mean more than one of something are **plural** words. Write these words. Beside them write their plural spelling words.

line **time** **name** **night**

line lines

time times

name names

night nights

3. What letter do we add to many words to make them plural?

s

4. Name these pictures.

dress

dresses

What two letters do we add to **dress** to spell **dresses**?

es

5. Write **bush** and **kiss.** Beside them write their plural spelling words.

bush bushes

kiss kisses

6. Write **house.** Write its plural.

house houses

What letter do we drop from the end of **house** to add **es**?

e

Since the suffix in *houses* is a new syllable, we say that the suffix is *-es* rather than only *-s*.

7. Write **baby** and **party.** Beside them write their plural spelling words.

baby babies

party parties

To add **es,** you changed **y** to i.

LESSON 15

See Introductions, page T16;
Test Sentences, page T25.

Purpose
To teach spelling verbs with the *-ed* suffix.

hunted
started
helped
played
stayed
washed
worked
missed
talked
turned
rained
snowed

PART A

Which spelling words have these meanings?

1. Looked for
2. Began
3. Spoke with the mouth
4. Did not go away

1. hunted
2. started
3. talked
4. stayed

Which spelling word fits best in each sentence?

5. Mother ——— hard cleaning the house.
6. Aunt Martha ——— us work all day.
7. I tried to catch it, but I ——— it.
8. We ——— with our trucks and dolls.
9. After it ———, we made a snowman.
10. We splashed in puddles after it ———.

5. worked
6. helped
7. missed
8. played
9. snowed
10. rained

PART B

1. Write these words. Beside them write the spelling words that are formed from these words.

talk **start** **wash**
turn **help** **miss**

talk	talked
turn	turned
start	started
help	helped
wash	washed
miss	missed

2. What two letters did you add to each word to make it mean that something already happened?

ed

The letters **ed** added to the end of a word are called a **suffix.**

3. Write these words. Then write them as they were before **ed** was added.

played **snowed** **hunted** **worked**

played	play
snowed	snow
hunted	hunt
worked	work

4. Write **stay, rain,** and **seem.** Beside them write other words by adding the suffix **ed** to the word.

stay	stayed
rain	rained
seem	seemed

See Introductions, page T16;
Test Sentences, page T25.

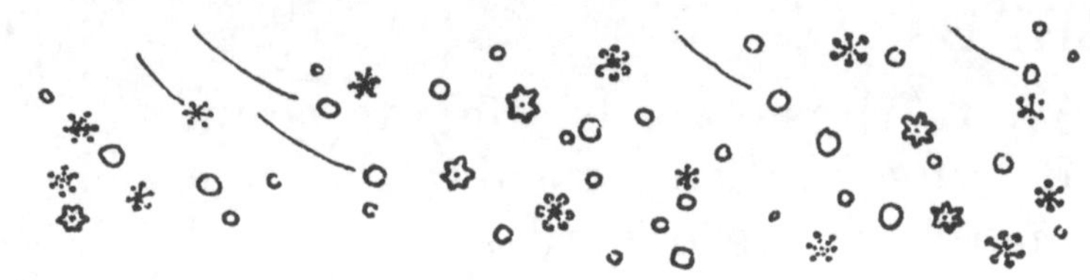

Purpose
To teach spelling verbs with the *-ing* suffix.

PART A

reading
singing
falling
telling
waiting
saying
doing
snowing
sending
fishing
running
putting

1. We are singing a new song.
2. Mother is telling us what to do.
3. It is snowing big white flakes.
4. Rain is falling from the clouds.
5. I am putting flowers into a jar.
6. The clock is not running anymore.
7. Are you doing your work well?
8. We were waiting for you to come.

PART B

1. Write these words. Beside them write the spelling words that are formed from these words.

tell	do	send
fish	say	fall

tell — telling

fish — fishing

do — doing

say — saying

send — sending

fall — falling

2. What three letters did you add to each word? ing

The letters **ing** added to the end of a word are called a **suffix.**

3. Write **reading, singing,** and **snowing.** Then write them as they were before **ing** was added.

reading — read

singing — sing

snowing — snow

4. Write **wait** and **grow.** Beside them write other words by adding **ing.**

wait — waiting

grow — growing

5. Write **run** and **put.** Circle **n** and **t** in the words you write.

run — put

6. Which spelling words are **ing** forms of **run** and **put**?

running — putting

Circle **nn** and **tt** in the words you wrote. The **n** and **t** were doubled.

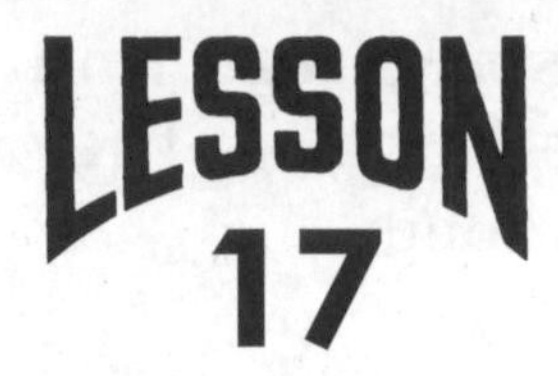

LESSON 17

See Introductions, page T17;
Test Sentences, page T25.

Purpose
To teach pupils to say and spell words by syllables.

wood
wagon
hung
any
began
father
mother
list
eating
after
Amen
Jesus

PART A

1. We say it at the end of a prayer.
2. It has wheels.
3. He is God's Son.
4. We get it from trees.
5. It means "started."
6. It means the opposite of **before.**

1. Amen
2. wagon
3. Jesus
4. wood
5. began
6. after

Which spelling words fit in these sentences?

7. I ——— my coat on the first hook.
8. Write all the names in a ———.
9. Can you see ——— stars?
10. The cattle are ——— grain.

7. hung
8. list
9. any
10. eating

PART B

1. Say these words as you write them.

at **duck** **nest** **swim**

at nest

duck swim

Hear only one vowel sound in each word. Circle **a, u, e,** and **i** in the words you wrote.

Each word has one syllable.

2. Say these words as you write them.

garden **kittens** **began** **thanking**

garden began

kittens thanking

Hear two vowel sounds in every word.

Each word has two syllables.

3. Write these words in syllables as they are here. Leave a space between the syllables.

gar den **kit tens**
be gan **thank ing**

gar den be gan

kit tens thank ing

4. In each of these words, we hear only one vowel sound. Each word has only one syllable. Write them.

hung **list** **wood** **eat**

hung wood

list eat

5. In each of these words, we hear two vowel sounds. Write the words, and leave a space between the syllables.

wag on **an y** **af ter**
fa ther **moth er** **eat ing**
A men **Je sus**

wag on moth er

fa ther Je sus

A men af ter

any eat ing

Purpose
To view concepts taught in Lessons 13–17.

No new concepts are introduced. Pupils can begin right away to do the exercises.

If a pupil's work in any exercise is poor, refer to the lesson in which the concept was taught. Reteach and give more practice.

See suggested test words and sentences, page T28.

13	14	15	16	17
roads	names	hunted	reading	wood
seats	times	started	singing	wagon
trains	nights	helped	falling	hung
arms	cows	played	telling	any
trees	lines	stayed	waiting	began
birds	bushes	washed	saying	father
boys	houses	worked	doing	mother
girls	kisses	missed	snowing	list
bees	baby	talked	sending	eating
heads	babies	turned	fishing	after
rooms	party	rained	running	Amen
beds	parties	snowed	putting	Jesus

PART A REVIEW

Fill in the puzzle with words from Lessons 13–17 that have these meanings. Print one letter in each block.

Pupils should print puzzle answers in all capital letters.

1. Insects that can sting
2. A very young child
3. The Son of God
4. Made clean with water
5. Falling in white flakes from the sky
6. Moving the legs fast to go somewhere
7. Buildings in which people live
8. Started
9. Animals that give milk
10. Things to sleep on

PART B REVIEW

1. Add **s** to make these words plural.

train **girl** **tree** **seat**

trains trees

girls seats

2. Add **es** to make these plural.

kiss **bush**

kisses bushes

3. Write **baby** and **party.** Write the spelling words that are their plurals.

baby babies

party parties

4. Add **ed** to these words.

turn **snow** **start** **work**

turned started

snowed worked

5. Add **ing** to these words.

wait **tell** **do** **eat**

waiting doing

telling eating

6. Which spelling words have **ing** added to **run** and **put**? Circle **nn** and **tt** in the words you write.

running putting

7. Write these one-syllable words.

birds **hung** **list** **rooms**

birds list

hung room

8. Write these two-syllable words with a space between the syllables.

wag on **A men**
hunt ed **send ing**

wag on A men

hunt ed send ing

LESSON 19

See Introductions, page T17;
Test Sentences, page T25.

Purpose
To teach common spellings of the /ā/ and /ē/ sounds.

table
gate
free
leaf
away
may
key
asleep
afraid
money
meal
mail

PART A

1. Two letters came in the mail.

2. This leaf fell from the tree.

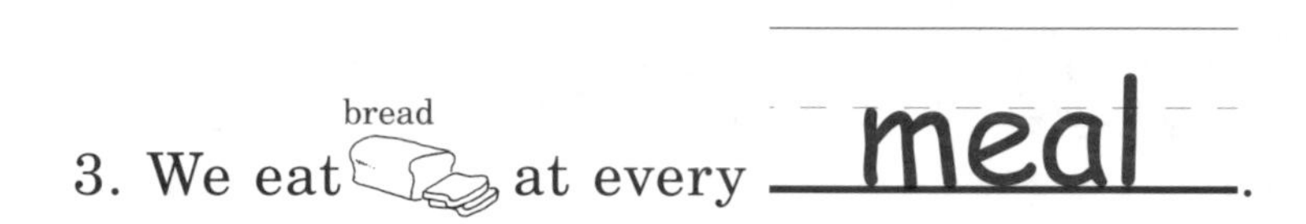

3. We eat bread at every meal.

4. Open the lock with a key.

5. Set the plates on the table.

6. Mother keeps money in her purse.

7. I am afraid of the lions.

8. We went away in the automobile.

PART B

1. Which spelling words name these pictures?

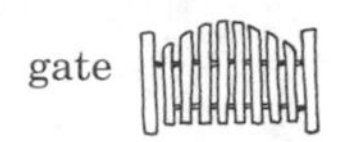

gate table

In the words you wrote, hear the same long vowel sound as in cake. In which other spelling words can you hear the long vowel sound in ?

away afraid

may mail

2. Which spelling words have this vowel sound spelled **ai**?

afraid mail

Which have this sound spelled **ay**?

away may

3. Write **table** in two syllables like this: **ta ble.** The letter **a** spells the long vowel sound.

ta ble

4. Which other spelling word has an **a** and then **e** at the end, like in **cake**?

gate

5. Which words name these pictures?

leaf key

In the words you wrote, hear the same long vowel sound as in tree.
In which other spelling words can you hear the long vowel sound in ?

free money

asleep meal

6. Which spelling words have this vowel sound spelled **ee**?

free asleep

Which have this sound spelled **ea**?

leaf meal

Which have this sound spelled **ey**?

key money

LESSON 20

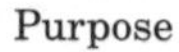

See Introductions, page T18;
Test Sentences, page T25.

Purpose
To teach common spellings of the /ī/ and /ō/ sounds.

PART A

1. Look until you **find** the cat.
2. I wear my coat when it is **cold**.
3. Did the wind **blow** your cap away?
4. The stars give **light** at night.
5. The boy plays with his toy **boat**.
6. Long **ago** there were no automobiles.
7. The horse jumped **over** the fence.
8. Our dog is blind in one **eye**.

PART B

1. Which spelling words name these pictures?

light / eye

light — eye

In the words you wrote, hear the same long vowel sound as in  kite. In which other spelling words can you hear the long vowel sound in kite?

find — buy

fight — by

2. Write the spelling words that have these spellings for the long vowel sound in kite.

i find — y by

uy buy

eye eye

igh fight — light

3. Say  rope and coat.

Listen for the long vowel sound.

In which spelling words can you hear the same long vowel sound as in rope and coat?

blow — over

boat — own

ago — cold

4. Write the spelling words that have these spellings for the long vowel sound in rope and coat.

oa boat

ow blow — own

o ago — cold

over

See Introductions, page T18;
Test Sentences, page T25.

Purpose
To teach common spellings of the /oo/ and /o͞o/ sounds.

took
cook
full
Jew
you
food
moon
looked
shoot
shoe
pushed
who

PART A

1. You wear it on your foot.
2. It shines in the nighttime sky.
3. We eat this.
4. It is another name for a Hebrew person.
5. This means "a person who prepares food."
6. It means the opposite of **empty.**
7. It means the opposite of **pulled.**
8. You did this with your eyes.

1. shoe
2. moon
3. food
4. Jew
5. cook
6. full
7. pushed
8. looked

9. God took Elijah to heaven.

10. We are glad that you are well.

PART B

1. Say the names of these pictures. Listen to the vowel sounds.

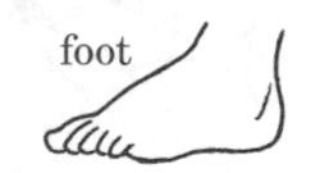

Write **book** and **foot.** In both words the vowel sound is spelled **oo.**

book

foot

2. Say the names of these pictures. Listen to the vowel sounds.

Is this the same vowel sound that you hear in **book** and **foot?**

no

Write **spoon** and **school.** In both words the vowel sound is spelled **oo.**

spoon school

3. Five spelling words have the same vowel sound that you hear in **book** and **foot.** Which three words have this vowel sound spelled **oo**?

took looked

cook

Now write **full** and **pushed.**

full pushed

What one letter spells the vowel sound in these words?

u

4. Seven spelling words have the same vowel sound that you hear in **spoon** and **school.** Which words have this vowel sound spelled **oo**?

food shoot

moon

5. Say **Jew, you, shoe,** and **who.** Hear the same vowel sound as in **spoon** and **school.** Now write the words to show how this sound is spelled.

o who **ew** Jew

ou you

oe shoe

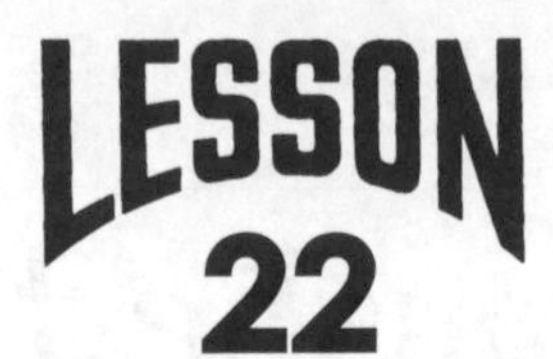

See Introductions, page T18;
Test Sentences, page T26.

Purpose
To teach spelling verbs with the *-s* suffix.

likes
takes
sees
helps
begins
needs
turns
goes
plays
stands
lives
gets

PART A

1. Which spelling words could fit in this sentence?

Mary Ann ——— the yellow cat.

likes needs
takes turns
sees gets
helps

2. Which spelling word means the opposite of **comes**? Which means the opposite of **ends**?

goes begins

3. A child does this with toys.
4. This word means "is upright on one's feet."

3. plays 4. stands

PART B

Copy the boldface words.

1. I **see** two stars. He **sees** three.

see sees

2. We **like** peas. Leon **likes** peas.

like likes

3. You may **begin** when she **begins.**

begin begins

4. They **live** where Uncle Paul **lives.**

live lives

5. If I **stand** up, the dog **stands** up.

stand stands

6. The way they **play** the game is different from how Doris **plays** it.

play plays

7. The little wheel will **turn** when the big wheel **turns.**

turn turns

8. Dennis and Roger **get** blue pencils. Ruth **gets** a yellow one.

get gets

9. I **need** you. She **needs** you too.

need needs

10. Will it **help** you? It **helps** me.

help helps

11. What letter did you always add to the first word to spell the second word?

s

12. Write **take.** Then write another word by adding **s.**

take takes

13. Write these boldface words.
We **go** to the store on Friday. Aunt Helen **goes** on Saturday.

go goes

What two letters are added to **go** to spell **goes**?

es

LESSON 23

See Introductions, page T19;
Test Sentences, page T26.

Purpose
To teach common spellings of the /ėr/ sound.

first
burn
words
learn
pearl
herself
were
working
under
paper
yesterday
never

PART A

1. It means the opposite of **last.**
2. It means the opposite of **above.**
3. It means the opposite of **always.**
4. It means the opposite of **tomorrow.**
5. Fire can do this to wood.
6. You can write on this with a pencil.

1. first
2. under
3. never
4. yesterday
5. burn
6. paper

Which spelling words fit in these sentences?

7. We are learning to spell many ——.
8. See the men —— on the roof.
9. Shepherds —— watching their sheep in the field.
10. We —— to add numbers in school.

7. words
8. working
9. were
10. learn

PART B

1. Say the names of these pictures.

Hear the **ėr** sound in every name. Write **fern, shirt, worm,** and **church.**

fern   worm

shirt   church

2. Write the picture names that have these spellings for the **ėr** sound.

er fern

ir shirt

or worm

ur church

3. Which spelling word has the **ėr** sound spelled **ere**?

were

4. Which spelling words have the **ėr** sound spelled **er** like in **fern**?

herself   yesterday

under   never

paper

5. Which spelling words have the **ėr** sound spelled **or** like in **worm**?

words   working

6. Which spelling words have the **ėr** sound spelled **ir** and **ur**?

first   burn

7. Find two spelling words that have the **ėr** sound spelled **ear.**

learn   pearl

8. Write **her** and **bird.** Circle **er** and **ir** in the words you write.

her   bird

Purpose
To view concepts taught in Lessons 19–23.

No new concepts are introduced. Pupils can begin right away to do the exercises.

If a pupil's work in any exercise is poor, refer to the lesson in which the concept was taught. Reteach and give more practice.

See suggested test words and sentences, page T28.

19	20	21	22	23
table	find	took	likes	first
gate	light	cook	takes	burn
free	blow	full	sees	words
leaf	boat	Jew	helps	learn
away	fight	you	begins	pearl
may	eye	food	needs	herself
key	ago	moon	turns	were
asleep	over	looked	goes	working
afraid	own	shoot	plays	under
money	cold	shoe	stands	paper
meal	buy	pushed	lives	yesterday
mail	by	who	gets	never

PART A REVIEW

Fill in the puzzle with words from Lessons 19–23 that have these meanings. Print one letter in each block.

Pupils should print puzzle answers in all capital letters.

1. A part of the body that helps a person to see
2. Something worn on the foot
3. Before any others
4. Fearful; scared
5. Doing a task or job
6. Her own self
7. Not awake
8. Not ever
9. A light in the nighttime sky
10. A tool that opens locks

PART B REVIEW

1. In each blank write a picture name in which the long **a** sound is spelled with the letter shown. The picture names are in Lesson 19.

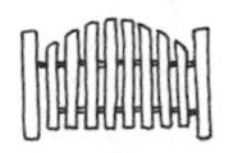 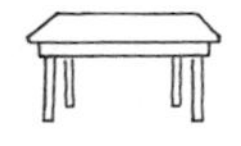 

a table **ai** mail

a-e gate

2. In each blank write a picture name in which the long **e** sound is spelled with the letters shown. The picture names are in Lesson 19.

 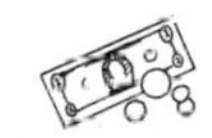 

ey money

ea leaf

ea meal

3. Write words from this group to show some different spellings of the long **o** sound.

blow **over** **boat**

o over

oa boat

ow blow

4. Write these words that show some ways to spell the **o͞o** sound.

you **who** **Jew** **food**

you Jew

who food

5. Write these words that show some ways to spell the **ėr** sound.

burn **yesterday** **learn** **words**

burn learn

yesterday words

6. Add the suffix **s** to these words.

begin **stand** **live** **like**

begins lives

stands likes

LESSON 25

See Introductions, page T19;
Test Sentences, page T26.

Purpose
To teach common spellings of the /k/ sound.

kind
coat
back
seek
kick
lakes
socks
ducks
block
cared
cleaning
brick

PART A

1. They like to swim in water.
2. Some animals do this with their feet.
3. It is the opposite of **front.**
4. This means "to look for."

1. ducks
3. back
2. kick
4. seek

5. Which spelling words could fit in this sentence?

I will wear my ——— today.

coat
socks

Which spelling words fit in these sentences?

6. The girls are ——— the dirty floor.
7. We try to be ——— to everybody.
8. Grandmother ——— for us while Mother was ill.
9. Geese and ducks swim on the ———.

6. cleaning
8. cared
7. kind
9. lakes

PART B

1. Say the names of these pictures. Listen for the first sound in each word.

The words **kite** and **cake** begin with the **k** sound. Which word begins with the **k** sound spelled **k**?

kite

Which word begins with the **k** sound spelled **c**?

cake

2. Which spelling words begin with the **k** sound spelled **k** like in **kite**?

kind   kick

3. Which spelling words begin with the **k** sound spelled **c** like in **cake**?

coat   cleaning

cared

4. Say the names of these pictures. Listen for the last sound in each word.

truck   clock

Write **truck** and **clock.**

truck   clock

5. In **truck** and **clock,** what two letters spell the **k** sound at the end of the word?

ck

6. Which spelling words end with the **k** sound spelled **ck**?

back   block

kick   brick

7. Which spelling words ended with **ck** before the suffix **s** was added?

socks   ducks

8. Find one spelling word that ends with the **k** sound spelled **k.** Find one spelling word that has **k** after a long **a** sound.

seek   lakes

9. Change the first letter in these words to the **k** sound spelled **c.** Write the words you make.

looking   **dry**

cooking   cry

See Introductions, page T19;
Test Sentences, page T26.

Purpose
To teach common spellings of the /s/ sound.

soft
sorry
nice
place
pass
talks
swing
city
last
stick
ice
once

PART A

1. It means the opposite of **first.**
2. It means the opposite of **hard.**
3. This is frozen water.
4. We should feel this way if we disobey.
5. Buildings are close together in this.
6. This word means "one time."
7. This word means "speaks."
8. It is a long, thin piece of wood.
9. People sit on this and move back and forth.
10. We do this with dishes of food at the table.

1. last
2. soft
3. ice
4. sorry
5. city
6. once
7. talks
8. sticks
9. swing
10. pass

PART B

1. Say the names of these pictures. Listen for the first sound in each word.

saw  socks 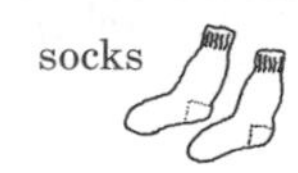

The words **saw** and **socks** begin with the **s** sound. What letter spells this sound?

2. Which spelling words begin with the **s** sound spelled **s** like in **socks**?

swing

sorry

stick

3. Which spelling word begins with the **s** sound spelled **c** like in **center**?

4. Say the names of these pictures. Listen for the last sound in each word.

dress  mice 

Write **dress** and **mice.**

dress

mice

5. What two letters spell the **s** sound at the end of **dress**?

6. Find a spelling word that ends with **ss.**

pass

7. What two letters spell the **s** sound at the end of **mice**?

ce

8. Write the spelling words that end with **ce.**

nice

ice

place

once

9. Write **last** and **talks.** Circle the **s** in the words you write.

last

talks

10. Write these words. Beside them write other words by changing the first letter to **s.**

fix **hide**

fix

six

hide

side

See Introductions, page T20;
Test Sentences, page T26.

Purpose
To teach common spellings of the /hw/ and /w/ sounds.

when
where
wind
wild
warm
woods
what
why
win
walking
while
wake

PART A

1. A cold wind is blowing.

2. My sweater keeps me warm.

3. In the woods are tall trees.

4. Someone will win the game.

5. Are we walking too fast?

6 Tigers are wild animals.

7. Which spelling words could fit in this sentence?
_____ are you going?

when where why

PART B

1. Name these pictures. Listen for the first sound in each word.

wagon

Write **window** and **wagon.** Circle the first **w** in each word you write.

window

2. Name these pictures. Listen for the first two sounds in each word.

Write **wheel** and **whale.** Circle **wh** in the words you write.

wheel

3. Which spelling words begin with the same sound that begins [wagon]?

wind win

wild walking

warm wake

woods

4. Which spelling words begin with the same sound that begins [wheel]?

when why

where while

what

5. Write these words. Beside them write other words by changing the first letter to **w.**

day he sell fishing talks

day way

he we

sell well

fishing wishing

talks walks

LESSON 28

See Introductions, page T20;
Test Sentences, page T26.

Purpose
To teach the use of the *-er* and *-est* suffixes to form words that compare.

higher
highest
bigger
dark
warmer
harder
larger
much
more
most
better
best

PART A

Write spelling words that mean the opposite of these words.

1. softer
2. lower
3. light
4. cooler
5. lowest
6. worse
7. worst
8. less

1. harder
2. higher
3. dark
4. warmer
5. highest
6. better
7. best
8. more

9. Which words mean the opposite of **smaller**?

bigger larger

10. The Bible is the ——— Book of all.
11. We love God ——— of all.

10. best
11. most

PART B

1. Write **warm** and **hard.** Beside them write spelling words that are forms of these words.

warm warmer

hard harder

What two letters are added as a suffix to **warm** and **hard**?

er

2. What spelling words are forms of **high**?

higher highest

What suffixes are added to **high**?

er est

3. Write **dark.** Then write other words by adding **er** and **est.**

dark darkest

darker

4. Write **big.** Write the spelling word that is a form of **big.**

big bigger

Circle **g** and **gg** in the words.

5. Write **large.** Write the spelling word that is a form of **large.**

large larger

Circle the **e** in **large** that you dropped to add **er.**

6. Write **much, more,** and **most.**

Our town had much rain.

Frytown had more rain than we did. Of all the places we heard about, Oakland had the most rain.

7. Write **better** and **best.**

Love is better than gold.

Jesus is our best friend.

See Introductions, page T20;
Test Sentences, page T27.

Purpose
To give practice in spelling words with double consonants.

spell
happy
kettle
hidden
across
add
apples
called
fell
dinner
off
still

PART A

1. These grow on trees.
2. We cook food in this.
3. You do this to numbers to find the sum.
4. This names a meal.
5. It means the opposite of **on.**
6. This word describes a thing that you cannot see.
7. It describes a thing that is not moving.
8. You feel this way when you do your work well.
9. You do this when you tell what letters make a word.
10. It means "from one side to the other."

1. apples
2. kettle
3. add
4. dinner
5. off
6. hidden
7. still
8. happy
9. spell
10. across

PART B

This is the first place that the term *double consonants* is used in this book. *Double* means "two." Double consonants are two like consonants side by side.

1. Write **all.** Circle **ll** in the word you write. Then write the spelling words that end with **ll.** Circle **ll** in these words too.

2. Which spelling words end with **ss, dd,** and **ff**? Circle the double consonants in the words you write.

across

3. Write **call.** Then write the spelling word that is a form of **call.** Circle the double consonants in both words.

4. Write **hide.** Then write the spelling word that is a form of **hide.** Circle **d** and **dd.**

hidden

5. In which spelling words do you see the double consonants **pp, nn,** and **tt**?

happy dinner

apples kettle

6. Say the words that you wrote in exercise 5. Hear two syllables in each word.

Write the words again. Put a dot between the syllables as shown in this word. **hap • py**
Divide each of the words between the double consonants.

hap•py din•ner

ap•ples ket•tle

7. Write only the words from this group that have double consonants.

bring **funny** **hall**
carry **card** **rabbits**

carry hall

funny rabbits

Purpose
To review concepts taught in Lessons 25–29.

No new concepts are introduced. Pupils can begin right away to do the exercises.

If a pupil's work in any exercise is poor, refer to the lesson in which the concept was taught. Reteach and give more practice.

See suggested test words and sentences, page T28.

25	26	27	28	29
kind	soft	when	higher	spell
coat	sorry	where	highest	happy
back	nice	wind	bigger	kettle
seek	place	wild	dark	hidden
kick	pass	warm	warmer	across
lakes	talks	woods	harder	add
socks	swing	what	larger	apples
ducks	city	why	much	called
block	last	win	more	fell
cared	stick	walking	most	dinner
cleaning	ice	while	better	off
brick	once	wake	best	still

PART A REVIEW

Fill in the puzzle with words from Lessons 25–29 that have these meanings. Print one letter in each block.

Pupils should print puzzle answers in all capital letters.

1. Frozen water
2. One time
3. Glad
4. A kind of fruit
5. Farthest from the ground
6. Removing dirt
7. Going somewhere by moving the legs
8. A meal people eat
9. Many trees close together
10. After all the others

PART B REVIEW

1. The letter that spells the **k** sound is missing in these words. Write the words correctly.

-ick -ettle -alled
-oat -ind -ared

kick kind

coat called

kettle cared

2. These words end with the **k** sound. Write the words correctly.

ba-- bri-- sti--
dar- see- blo--

back seek

dark stick

brick block

3. These words begin with the **s** sound. Write the words correctly.

-pell -oft -ity -orry

spell city

soft sorry

4. Write **place, nice, pass,** and **across.** Hear the **s** sound. Circle **ce** or **ss** in the words.

place pass

nice across

5. Write these. Begin them with **w** or **wh.** -en -ind -y -arm

when why

wind warm

6. Add **er** and **est** to **hard.**

harder hardest

7. Write **hidden** and **still.** Circle the double consonants.

hidden still

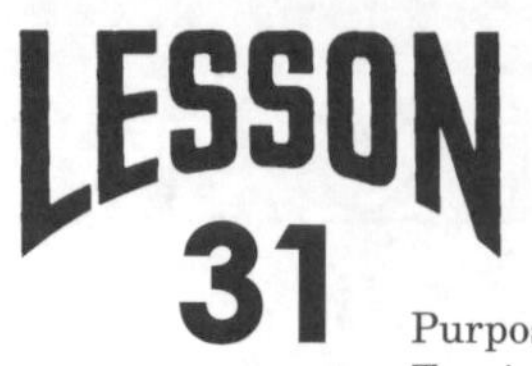

See Introductions, page T21;
Test Sentences, page T27.

Purpose
To give practice in forming plural nouns by adding *-s* and *-es*.

stars
songs
laws
doors
dishes
tests
yards
stores
wings
eyes
cards
flies

PART A

Write a spelling word that could fit with each group of words below.

1. Plates, spoons, cups
2. Mouth, nose, ears
3. Windows, roof, walls
4. Sun, moon
5. Poems, stories
6. Rules, commandments
7. Bees, grasshoppers, beetles
8. Feathers, beak

1. dishes
2. eyes
3. doors
4. stars
5. songs
6. laws
7. flies
8. wings

9. Groceries are sold in grocery ———.
10. Janet received three birthday ———.

9. stores
10. cards

PART B

Pupils studied plural nouns in Lessons 13 and 14.

1. Write **dog** and **dogs** below the correct pictures.

dog dogs

2. Write **song** and **card.** Then write the spelling words that mean "more than one song" and "more than one card."

song songs

card cards

3. What letter can be added to a word to mean more than one?

s

4. Write these words. Beside them write their plural spelling words.

door	law	eye	store
star	yard	test	wing

door doors

star stars

law laws

yard yards

eye eyes

test tests

store stores

wing wings

5. Write **dish.** Write a word that means "more than one dish" by adding **es.**

dish dishes

6. Write **fly.** Write the spelling word that means "more than one fly."

fly flies

In the words you wrote, circle **y** and **ies.**

LESSON 32

See Introductions, page T21;
Test Sentences, page T27.

Purpose
To give practice in forming verbs with *-ed* and *-ing*.

PART A

learned
asked
passing
owned
burning
needed
riding
loving
liked
kicked
holding
carried

1. Father is burning the trash. 

2. The teacher asked a question.

3. Are you holding it carefully? 

4. Who is riding the bicycle?

5. The horse kicked and ran. 

6. I learned to spell many words.

7. The sad dog needed a home. 

8. We carried the boxes for him. 

PART B

Pupils studied *-ed* verbs in Lesson 15 and *-ing* verbs in Lesson 16.

1. Write spelling words that are forms of **need** and **kick.**

needed kicked

What suffix ends the spelling words that you wrote? ed

2. Write spelling words that are forms of **burn** and **hold.**

burning holding

What suffix ends the spelling words that you wrote? ing

3. Write the first four spelling words in the list. Beside them write the words as they were before the suffixes were added.

learned learn

asked ask

passing pass

owned own

4. Write **love, ride,** and **like.** Beside them write spelling words that are forms of these words.

love loving

ride riding

like liked

What letter did you drop to add the suffix? e

5. Write **carry** and **carried.**

carry carried

To add **ed** to **carry,** you changed the letter y to i.

See Introductions, page T22;
Test Sentences, page T27.

Purpose
To teach pupils to say and spell words by syllables.

water
pony
into
ring
many
filling
carries
storm
river
zoo
hands
upon

PART A

Write a spelling word that could fit with each group of words below.

1. Horse, donkey
2. Milk, juice, tea
3. Creek, lake, stream
4. Legs, feet, arms

1. pony
2. water
3. river
4. hands

5. Tigers, elephants, and monkeys make you think of the word ——.
6. Thunder, lighting, and rain make you think of the word ——.

5. zoo
6. storm

7. What word means almost the same as **circle**?
8. What word means opposite of **few**?
9. What word means opposite of **under?**
10. What word means opposite of **emptying**?

7. ring
8. many
9. upon
10. filling

PART B

Pupils studied syllables in lesson 17.

1. Say these words as you write them.

am **bells** **not** **nuts**

am not

bells nuts

Hear only one vowel sound in each word. Circle **a,** **e,** **o,** and **u** in the words you wrote.

Each word has one syllable.

2. Say these words as you write them.

calling **brother** **given** **around**

calling given

brother around

Hear two vowel sounds in every word.

Each word has two syllables.

3. Write these words in syllables as they are here. Leave a space between the syllables.

call ing **broth er**
giv en **a round**

call ing giv en

broth er a round

4. In each of these words, we hear only one vowel sound. Each word has only one syllable. Write them.

ring **storm** **zoo** **hands**

ring zoo

storm hands

5. In each of these words, we hear two vowel sounds. Write the words, and leave a space between the syllables.

po ny **wa ter** **man y**
fill ing **riv er** **car ries**
up on **in to**

po ny riv er

fill ing in to

up on man y

wa ter car ries

Purpose
To review concepts taught in Lessons 31–33.

No new concepts are introduced. Pupils can begin right away to do the exercises.

If a pupil's work in any exercise is poor, refer to the lesson in which the concept was taught. Reteach and give more practice.

See suggested test words and sentences, page T29.

31	32	33
stars	learned	water
songs	asked	pony
laws	passing	into
doors	owned	ring
dishes	burning	many
tests	needed	filling
yards	riding	carries
stores	loving	storm
wings	liked	river
eyes	kicked	zoo
cards	holding	hands
flies	carried	upon

PART A REVIEW

Fill in the puzzle with words from Lessons 31–33 that have these meanings. Print one letter in each block. Pupils should print puzzle answers in all capital letters.

1. Place where different kinds of animals are kept
2. Parts of your body that help you to see
3. Lights in the nighttime sky
4. Buildings where things are sold
5. Take from one place to another
6. Took from one place to another
7. Hit with the foot
8. A liquid that we drink
9. A kind of animal
10. Rules

PART B REVIEW

1. Write **hand, song,** and **river.** Beside each one write its plural form by adding **s.**

hands hands

song songs

river rivers

2. Write these words. Beside each one write it as it was before **s** was added.

doors **storms** **yards**

doors door

storms storm

yards yard

3. What spelling words are the plural forms of **dish** and **fly**?

dishes flies

4. Write spelling words by adding **ed** or **ing** to these words.

hold **learn** **fill**
need **love** **ask**

holding loving

needed filling

learned asked

5. Write these one-syllable words.

ring **wings** **cards** **owned**

ring cards

wings owned

6. Write these two-syllable words. Leave a space between the syllables.

burn ing **man y** **rid ing** **in to**

burn ing rid ing

man y in to